Myths of Oz

MEDIA AND POPULAR CULTURE

A series of critical books

Series Editor: David Thorburn, Director of Film and Media Studies and Professor of Literature, Massachusetts Institute of Technology

Media and Popular Culture presents original interpretive studies devoted to various forms of contemporary culture, with emphasis on media texts, audiences, and institutions. Its goal is the creation of a fruitful dialogue between recent strains of feminist, semiotic, and marxist cultural study and older forms of humanistic and social-scientific scholarship. The series is explicitly eclectic in its theoretical assumptions and committed to a discourse that is intellectually rigorous yet accessible and lucid.

MYTHS OF OZ

Reading Australian Popular Culture

John Fiske   Bob Hodge   Graeme Turner

Boston
ALLEN & UNWIN
London   Sydney   Wellington

Copyright © 1987 by John Fiske, Bob Hodge and Graeme Turner
All rights reserved.

Allen & Unwin, Inc.
8 Winchester Place, Winchester, MA 01890, USA.

The U.S. Company of
Unwin Hyman Ltd

P.O. Box 18, Park Lane, Hemel Hempstead, Herts HP2 4TE, UK
40 Museum Street, London WC1A 1LU, UK
37/39 Queen Elizabeth Street, London SE1 2QB, UK

Allen & Unwin Australia Pty Ltd,
8 Napier Street, North Sydney, NSW 2060, Australia

Allen & Unwin (New Zealand) Ltd, in association with the Port Nicholson Press Ltd
Private Bag, Wellington, New Zealand

Library of Congress Cataloging-in-Publication Data

Fiske, John.
  Myths of Oz.

  (Media and popular culture; 2)
  Bibliography: p.
  Includes index.
  1. Australia—Popular culture.   I. Hodge, Bob (Robert
Ian Vere)   II. Turner, Graeme.   III. Title.   IV. Series.
DU107.F53 1987   994.06′3   87-12648
ISBN 0-04-330391-9
ISBN 0-04-306005-6 (pbk.)

British Library Cataloguing in Publication Data

Fiske, John.
  Myths of Oz: reading Australian popular
  culture.
  1. Australia—Social life and customs
  I. Title   II. Hodge, Robert   III. Turner,
  Graeme
  994.06′3   DU107

  ISBN 0-04-330391-9
  ISBN 0-04-306005-6 Pbk

Set in 10½/12pt Stempel Garamond by Asco Trade Typesetting Ltd
Printed in Hong Kong

Contents

Illustrations

Introduction

We wrote this book out of a sense of puzzlement, which many Australians must feel about their country and its culture. From all sides we had been hearing the long-established, traditional criticism bewailing the lack of an Australian culture. Yet this wasn't at all how it felt for us as typical-enough denizens of Australia, living in this self-styled cultural desert, this culture which we're told does not exist. It wasn't that we saw nothing to criticise in Australian life and culture. But the Australia we lived in had a richness and diversity that was incompatible with the Australia of the culture critics.

We suspected that part of the problem came from opposing definitions of 'culture'. The Knocker tradition started from an elitist view of culture. It yearned for Australia to be seen as the Athens of the south, astounding European visitors with the number of masterpieces of art, music and literature. But there are other definitions of culture that are more populist and more comprehensive. These definitions see culture as concerned with the whole way of life of a people, their customs and rituals, their pastimes and pleasures, including not only the arts but also practices such as sport and going to the beach.

To us it seemed clearly an advance to acknowledge the vitality and interest of Australian popular culture. But the dichotomy still felt unsatisfactory. We didn't want to affirm everything in Australian popular life, any more than we wanted to reject high culture *in toto*. The contradictions we were aware of didn't seem to be situated exclusively between high culture and popular culture. Contradiction seems to be more endemic. It was present in both domains of culture. It was even something we saw in very particular aspects of the culture.

The only way we could make sense of these contradictions was to emphasise culture as itself dynamic, to see Australian culture not as a static collection of items but as a play of forces. We saw it as a set of ways of constructing meanings, not as specific objects or artefacts. In this view its meanings are not fixed and its values are not common. Even with such familiar cultural landmarks as the pub or the beach, the stereotype judgments ignore the creative role of the users of these cultural forms. We think they are best seen as sites where Australians construct (and deconstruct) a plenitude of meanings, using a multitude of practices—not a single meaning with a single value.

We came to the view that our greatest problem had been an unexamined belief in a monolithic Australian culture. Every previous attempt to pin it down in a single definition seemed to miss this most important point. Keith Hancock's *Australia*, Russel Ward's *Australian Legend*, Donald Horne's *Lucky Country*, Ronald Conway's *Great Australian Stupor* and Craig McGregor's *Profile of Australia* offer different definitions and prescriptions, but they all assume that that's what a book on Australian culture ought to be trying to do; they try to discover a single comprehensive and distinctive 'truth' about Australian society and the Australian character. This truth is then evaluated, with exhortations or forebodings assembled in the final chapter.

In our book we have no comprehensive definition of Australian culture, and instead we hope to offer a fruitful way of interpreting its various aspects. This takes the form of a series of particular '*readings*'. Through these readings we want to demonstrate the richness of meaning that can be found in Australian culture even at points where so many critics have tried to persuade their compatriots that the only meanings to be found are trivial or obnoxious.

The approach we adopted draws on an important tradition in cultural studies called semiotics: the study of systems of signs. We won't be giving a systematic or technical exposition of semiotics, and our readings stand or fall by their own merits, not by appeal to some theory. But some of the methods of semiotics are simple and accessible, yet powerful. One is the notion of 'reading' itself. In *Myths of Oz* we say we are 'reading' Australian culture. The analogy with reading books is a fruitful one. It encourages a close analysis of the kind that is normally reserved for literary texts, extending it to cultural products such as film and television and to cultural practices, rituals and behaviours.

'Culture' here is essentially the anthropologists' use of the term—the 'way of life' of a people, the constant and complex process by which meanings are made and shared amongst us. The *'texts'* through which this process works include deliberately constructed artefacts such as buildings, and they also include those things to which we normally attach little significance: the clothes we wear, the way we use our leisure, how we organise our daily lives. Culture in this sense is the result of the multifarious processes of making meanings for a society. These meanings may underpin the social structure and make it viable by winning people's consent to the social system. But the meanings may also express dissatisfaction with it, and act as an evolutionary rather than reactionary force.

Semiotic analysis, as we practise it, is another name for the study of the patterns of meaning by which a social group organises its life. This way of studying culture proceeds through what we call 'texts'. The idea of analysing key texts is a familiar one in literary studies, and to some extent our use of the notion is derived from that source. Our texts, too, are subjected to readings that can be detailed and complicated. They are drawn from everyday life though, and bear little relation to the privileged bearers of the great traditions of literary studies. These texts cannot stand alone. Their meanings are too pervasive and fluid. The readings are thus never final or definitive, but describe the production of meaning rather than the production of *the* meaning. Many of the texts we examine produce different meanings for different users, and the various meanings may compete or conflict. The meaning of the pub as a 'text', for instance, is different to the regulars in the front bar, the couples in the lounge, and the rock'n'roll fans who use it on weekends only. Culture does not grow out of the unity of a society but out of its divisions. It has to work to *construct* any unity that it has, rather than simply celebrate an achieved or natural harmony. Culture is a producer and re-producer of value systems and power relations, performing crucial ideological functions within Australia. In our discussion we will make no sharp distinction between the terms 'culture' and 'ideology'.

Our analysis of Australia focuses particularly on 'lived texts' (the pub, the beach, the shopping centre) where the meanings are often unconscious and implicit in various practices and forms of behaviour, yet decisive for an understanding of the society and the culture. Lived texts are more difficult to read than 'produced' texts (e.g. books, films, plays), and most cultural analysts ignore them. However, by reading them semiotically we can bring out the social and ideological forces which produced them, by examining their place within the whole cultural system. Most importantly, lived texts are closer to the generative centre of the culture process, for they arise directly from the material conditions of life.

We have done our best to trim academic theory out of our analyses, but we do need to explain a couple of terms now, as they will occur within the first few chapters. Essential to semiotics is the notion that communication—the generation and circulation of meaning between users of a language—is achieved by the same kind of system no matter what language or language-like activity (dress or gesture, for instance) is used. The basic unit of this system is the *sign*. A sign is simply anything, e.g. an object, sound, image, word or act, that has an accepted meaning for a person or group of people. Every sign has two aspects: the *signifier* (roughly, the carrier of meaning) including the form of the sign (e.g. a photo, an advertisement) and the *signified* (the mental concept to which the sign refers). Although both signifier and signified are united in the sign, we can talk about the two terms separately. So, we can talk about signifiers of Australianness, using the one term to describe the way different objects (words, photos, advertising images, the national anthem) refer to the same mental concept. The signified 'Australia' can be borne by a host of different signifiers—kangaroos, the flag, Alan Bond, the map, images of landscape, the Sydney Opera House, and so on. Advertisements frequently try to connect their products with the signified 'Australia', and they do this by selecting and combining signifiers of this 'Australia' within their ads. The meaning associated with the yacht *Australia II*, for instance, is connected with Swan Export in order to further define and locate a *meaning* of that beer within the culture.

In this example, the grouping of signifiers around a concept creates what Roland Barthes in his book *Mythologies* called a 'myth'. This is not a myth in the sense that it is untrue, but rather in the sense of a systematic organisation of signifiers around a set of connotations and meanings. The myth of Australia in the Swan beer commercial is composed of (among other things) signifiers of egalitarianism, the underdog, a dogged persistence and ultimate success. Such myths act as points of focus for the culture, and we will see them in action during the readings that follow.

Our readings are meant to reveal the processes, the languages, through which '*Australia*' is constructed. '*Australia*' thus can be seen as a system of meanings. This is not to say that it doesn't or shouldn't exist. On the contrary, it does exist, as a set of meanings, as a semiotic construct and as a political stance. The meanings which make up 'Australia' impinge on many aspects of our life. Our readings will show that the process of defining 'Australia' continues as a live issue. Our analysis of the beach and the home and the pub reveals change and contradictions, fundamental realignments of how Australians structure the significant places in their life. In our reading of the Sydney Opera House we see how the popular uses of a building can overturn and extend its intended function. A profound ambivalence towards Aboriginal culture can be seen in many parts of the dominant culture such as patterns of tourism. The cumulative result of our readings should be a sense of the way in which the possibilities offered by Australian popular culture are regulated—countered by an equally strong sense of the richness of possibilities that are contained within, and also threaten to explode, the boundaries described.

There are many individual Australias, and the concept of Australia exists only as long as we all agree on the commonalities between our individual versions. *Myths of Oz* has been a collaborative effort partly because we needed to retain a sense of the different ways in which Australianness is experienced and constructed and represented. But with our separate histories and experiences, we share an enthusiasm for Australian popular culture, and all three authors have contributed to all sections of the book, in a genuinely collaborative enterprise. The names on the cover are listed purely alphabetically, not in order of importance of contribution.

A great number of people have been confronted, interviewed, queried and consulted in the course of this book. Many of our colleagues in cultural studies throughout the country have provided generous and useful responses to work in progress. Our editor, John Tulloch, has been an especially enthusiastic goad to the completion of the book. Chris Turner and Pam Hodge offered criticisms and suggestions which have been incorporated into the final text. Bob Hodge's students at Murdoch University, and John Fiske and Graeme Turner's students at the Western Australian Institute of Technology, have operated as sources of information, useful scepticism and frank disbelief during the development of the material in this book. The authors acknowledge their contributions with thanks. Of our colleagues who have read the manuscript, Alan Mansfield deserves special thanks. Joyce Avraamides, and Rae Kelly's contributions extend far beyond their word-processing abilities: if all academics had the sort of help and enthusiasm that Rae and Joyce provide, academic life would be noticeably more productive.

For permission to use illustrations we owe acknowledgments to *Belle*; *Homes and Living*; News Ltd; John Fairfax and Sons; Richard Woldendorp; Michael Fitzjames; Philip Neilsen; the *Wanneroo Times*; the *Western Mail*; the *Sunday Times*; Murray Publishing, Sheraton Hotels and the collection of the Art Gallery of South Australia. Although every attempt has been made to trace the illustrations' sources, in a couple of instances we have not been successful. For this we apologise and would welcome claims for acknowledgment in subsequent editions.

1 The Pub

It may seem somewhat insulting to begin our reading of Australia in the pub. But Australians are both proud and ashamed of their enthusiasm for alcohol. The Australian image has had an alcohol problem from the earliest days of the colony, and pubs have interested the analysts of Australian culture for almost as long. On the one hand, they have proposed a nexus (bond or link) between one image of Australian masculinity and the huge consumption of beer, still regarding the pub as the beer-stained site of the notorious 'six o'clock swill'. On the other hand, populists defend the pub as the location of the authentic Australian values of mateship and egalitarianism. For Craig McGregor, 'drinking provides the focus of much Australian life . . . the pub has partly replaced the dance hall as a convivial gathering place for men and women'. He sees drinking as 'a determinedly egalitarian activity, the great social leveller— except for a Test Cricket crowd there is no more classless place in Australia than a hotel bar.' [p. 136] This (from *Profile of Australia*) was written in 1967. McGregor would want to modify this judgment now, partly because there have been significant changes in pub culture and drinking customs in the intervening two decades. Those changes and their underlying structures of meaning provide insight into important levels of Australian society.

Revolution at Surfers Paradise

Surfers Paradise isn't usually regarded as the most likely place for a revolution, but fortunately such an event was recorded in December, 1984. The famous Birdwatchers' Bar, the glass-walled vantage point in the centre of Surfers Paradise where men could watch, heckle and whistle at passing women, has gone, or rather, has been

1

Surfers loses a look of the past

By JOE PAYNE

SOME call it progress, others put it down to women's liberation. Some say it marks a return to decency and good sense; still others say it smacks of wowserism or puritanism.

In any event, Surfers Paradise acknowledged a significant social change last week. The famous — or infamous — Birdwatchers' Bar, a part of ockerish and chauvinist Australia for decades, is just not the same.

The drinking men can still look at the passing women. The point is that the women can't see the men looking. As one beer-bellied, blue-shorted drinker put it: "If the birds can't see you perving on them, where's the fun?"

What has put them off their game is the tinted glass which shields the women and young girls in bikinis from seeing and hearing the watchers as they move past the bar in the $50 million Surfers Paradise Centre, opened last Tuesday.

The Birdwatchers' Bar on the corner of Cavill Avenue is the only memento of the old Surfers Paradise Hotel and its Johnnie Walker tower facade which attracted visitors from across Australia for decades.

The new super centre, spreading across 2.3ha to the beach Esplanade with its spacious shopping plaza and skyscraper luxury accommodation, is among the most valuable real estate in Australia.

It also has a huge beer garden, but now it has a retractable roof on the first floor of the Cavill Avenue complex and four small boxes of tropical plants are the only sign of a "garden".

Developer Mr Ernie Kornhauser said he had placed his family's fortunes and futures on the line in the massive development he descibed as a heart transplant for the Gold Coast.

"It is not just my interests that are invested here, but virtually the whole accumulated wealth of my brother Jack, his family, my family and myself, earned over 35 years of extremely hard work," said Mr Kornhauser, who came to Australia as a displaced person from Poland in 1939 with next to nothing in his pocket. "I am proud to have created something that will give pleasure to millions of families for many years."

Bars, birds and change. Changes in the formal structure of pubs are connected with changes in the level of seriousness with which the needs of women are taken and the degree to which the pub is seen as entirely a masculine precinct. The compromise described in the renovation of the famous Birdwatchers' corner, may look like progress (and clearly the reporter sees it in this manner), but it leaves the basic position of the watchers unchanged. What it does is protect them from the accusation of sexism by allowing them to indulge in it privately. Still protecting the male, the pub's new windows transform him from predator to voyeur—an image of the change in male–female relations in recent years. While updated and civilised, the pub still employs many of the same ideological principles embedded in its origins.

transformed. The terms through which this event are grasped by reporter Joe Payne are all weighted with cultural meaning. First there is the opposition between present and past, implicitly invoking an immemorial tradition (of at least twenty years) ended by the harsh realities of the present. The article announces its alignment towards the traditional past in the headline—Surfers has 'lost' something by the change, not gained anything new.

In the past that is invoked by Payne, the problem both raised and solved by pubs is the relationship between men and women. The terms of this relationship, at the old-style Birdwatchers' Bar, were 'male chauvinist', as all analysts readily agree, though not all would use those precise words. The pub was a male preserve, matching male preserves in many other cultures. But though the male–male relationship is normally seen as primary in the domain of the pub, the activity of the old Birdwatchers' Bar is a revealing exaggeration. The satisfaction, for the drinker, was not simply 'perving'—a displaced sexuality—but also being seen to perve, by women who would know and pretend not to respond. What the drinker missed was not simply the aggression of perving (which he can still indulge in through the one-way glass) but the complicity of women with that asymmetrical male power. Male solidarity, then, provides not so much a positive value in its own right, but a barrier protecting male sexuality and aggression from female counter-aggression. The glib reference to 'women's liberation' in the report's first sentence is somewhat misleading, if it implies that the women's movement has been struggling for years to require men to look at women through one-way glass, but it does carry the obscure sense of male vulnerability to women that existed in the past as in the present. It was never the case that relations of man to man in a pub setting were offered as an autonomous and fully satisfying form of existence—real Australian males weren't homosexuals and were very disturbed at that accusation. What the Birdwatchers' Bar makes clear is the role of the pub world as a kind of anti-world, a bracketed space where the normative relationships of the real world were suspended or inverted, though only temporarily. Its cultural function was both to achieve that status and to control it; to limit it in place (the pub, not the home or workplace, or anywhere else) and time (the hours of business of the pub, whose opening and closing times are laid down).

The State, naturally, has always been concerned with regulation and control of this inherently antisocial activity and its legitimated sites. Australia stopped short of America's experiment with prohibition, and instead introduced six o'clock closing during the First World War. This upper limit, combined with a five o'clock end to the working day, created the legendary 'six o'clock swill', and this only slightly less repressive regulation lasted longer than prohibition, with effects on drinking customs in Australia that continue. In an interview in the American magazine *Rolling Stone* in 1984, the Australian rock band Men at Work regaled the reporter with memories of the swill in Melbourne, offering an apparently gratuitous account of local customs which it is highly unlikely that they were old enough to experience. This is the 'Legend of the Swill', with drinkers fighting for beers, vomiting and urinating where they stood in order to keep their places at the bar, tiles on the walls and floors, and lino-covered counters to lean against which could simply be hosed down after closing.

The six o'clock rule was repealed in New South Wales in the mid-1950s, and even later in some states, but as a myth it still has explanatory power about contemporary habits and conditions in pubs (as Men at Work recognised when they drew on it). Craig McGregor, again in *Profile of Australia*, had this to say:

> Once they were strictly utilitarian places, designed for hard drinking and nothing else: long, slops-wet bars which men could rest an elbow on as they drank standing up, lavatory-tiled floors and walls so they could be hosed down when the pub closed for the night, no chairs or tables to sit at, a couple of calendars pinned to the wall, a decrepit radio for listening to the races on Saturday afternoons, a large public bar, a small saloon bar, and tiny 'Ladies Lounge', and, so the publican hoped, a fierce-drinking clientele which didn't give the barmaids too much trouble by ordering fancy drinks. Most pubs are still like that, given over entirely to men in the bars, with faded old-fashioned beer posters in glass cases outside the swing doors and perhaps a chalk and black board counter lunch menu and a TV set jammed high in one corner of the bar as the only concessions to changing taste. [p. 136]

When he started the first long sentence with 'once', McGregor clearly thought he was going to contrast this utilitarian beastliness with something different and better, but by the time he finished the inventory he realised that not much had changed after all. There are signs of change, however, that qualify the dominance of the public bar and of an exclusively masculine pub culture. The growth of lounge bars and taverns and international-styled hotel bars has seen a real increase in numbers of women patrons. In Centrepoint Tavern in Sydney, for instance, one will see almost as many women as men on an average weeknight, many of them not accompanied by men. Yet such instances can still be seen as exceptions, whose significance is still read off from the dominant model. In spite of its seeming brutality, and claims that the social mores have radically changed, the traditional public bar retains its centrality and ubiquity, and rather than join either the knockers or the drinkers we must try to read it and understand the cultural necessity of its often puzzling features.

A Home Away From Home

The pub is a building, but more importantly it is a category of place, organised as one of a set of 'domains'. A domain in this sense is not simply a physical location. It is a social space, organised by a set of rules which specify who can be in it and what they can do. It also controls meanings: what meanings can be expressed and how, and how they will be interpreted.

Pubs have different functions in different communities. The role of a traditional country pub, for instance, grows out of a community with many characteristics different from those of urban populations. Limiting ourselves to contemporary metropolitan pubs, however, we can notice one initial classification in terms of location and function. There are, simply, city pubs and suburban pubs, with the majority in the suburbs. The temporal positioning of drinking in a typical day and week shows two peaks: one at lunchtime during the working day, and a larger one after work finishes, especially on a Friday night. The first peak is situated at an interface between work and work, and the second between work and home. The city pub is situated closer to the working place, the suburban pub to the home (although there are important class differences in places of working which we should not ignore, since they result in different kinds of pub and different kinds of pub culture). The pub is determined by relations to these two domains, the places of work and the home. Its function is to mediate their opposition by a complex set of repudiations and incorporations of both. So, on the one hand the pub can be called a 'home away from home', while on the other hand it can be seen as a major threat to domestic life. In fact one of the motives for the six o'clock closing was to protect the family home by ensuring that the husband spent his nights there (however incapacitated by the effects of the 'swill') rather than in the pub. Yet the interface with work relations is equally marked. The relationship with mates is a continuation of the unsatisfactory relations with others in the workplace, but transformed under better conditions. If the 'boss' joins 'the boys' at the pub it is now as an equal (almost) and as a mate, sharing a common male humanity. From these two relationships the pub gains its double character, as an anti-home and an anti-workplace.

Initially the classic pub format, so accurately described by Craig McGregor, reveals its status as an anti-home. This explains what is otherwise the most puzzling feature of pubs: their sheer drabness. The heart of the pub is the public bar, which is not only opposed to the saloon or lounge bar but even more to the domestic lounge room. We can list some contrasts:

Domestic lounge	Hotel bar
Ostentatious decor	Spartan, utilitarian decor
Carpet or rugs	Tiles
Plush seats/sofas	Bar stools, places to stand
Well lit	Poorly lit
Quiet	Noisy
Oriented to display	Oriented to use

In our discussion of the role of the lounge room in the suburban family home, in Chapter 2, we shall point out that it is public not private space, sacrificed to others, not for the self, even though it seems to be the self that gains the credit for the display. It is this kind of space that is most strongly repudiated by the public bar, in which self-display of this kind is specifically rejected in favour of an egalitarian ethos and private self-indulgence.

Essential here is the conception of social relations which the pub world exists to preserve and express. We can set up two lists again, as follows:

The domain of the pub. Despite renovations, the floor can still be hosed down at the end of the day, the occupants are still male, and the outside world is the cause of the retreat. Vinyl stools, laminex benches, tiled bars, dart boards and counter lunch menus are still the norm. In one of these bars, a TV set bore the admonition, 'To Be Used For Watching Sporting Events Only'. Diminished it may be as the dominant area in the pub these days, but its values are still preserved, and defended.

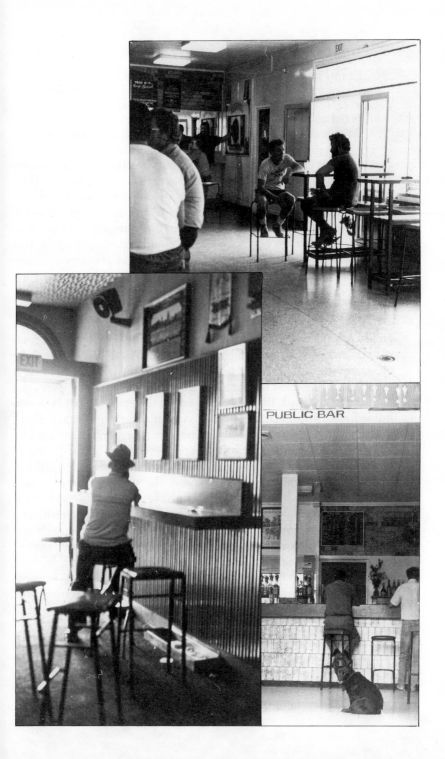

Domestic lounge	Hotel bar
Family and friends	Mates and acquaintances
Mixed sex	Single sex (plus barmaid)
Hierarchical	Non-hierarchical
Fixed and permanent relations	Temporary relations
Asymmetrical obligations	Symmetrical obligations

In this scheme we note that is not family relationships, especially the relationship of the husband and wife, that are repudiated here, so much as the repressive formality of the bourgeois family, in which intimacy and sexuality are suppressed as strongly, though differently, as in an all-male bar. It is in the lounge room that society asserts its benign control over the couple, imposing a male role of dominance which is qualified by a crushing set of obligations and duties, and a female role of domestic expertise and cheerful acquiescence in a life of service. It is the lounge room that the male escapes from, not the heart of the house—if it has one for him.

Instead of the fixed, oppressive hierarchical relations of the family lounge room, the public bar eschews hierarchy and permanence. It does have one obligation, or it did have: the 'shout', the obligation of every drinker to pay for his round in turn. Because it seems equal, it seems fair, though its equality is coercive: everyone is assumed to drink the same amount at the same speed. It is also immediate justice, not a nebulous system of deferred repayments, as when the hosts in the family home, having expended money and effort on entertainment for others, are invited back in due course to a similar occasion. Because the 'shout' is the main obligation imposed on drinkers, its refusal becomes the supreme crime against this specially constituted society. But the set of obligations are temporary, confined to the world of the pub, not tediously continuous like those of parents to children, for instance. This can make them seem irrational to an outsider. This can be seen in the response of the middle-class school teacher in the film *Wake in Fright*, to a truck driver who has invited him for a drink, and is refused: 'What's wrong with you people?' he asks. 'You can steal from you, rape your wife, but if you won't have a drink you're the worst in the world.'

A central figure who both links and opposes the pub and the domestic lounge is the barmaid. Like the wife, she is female. She fulfils the stereotyped female functions of happy service and provision of sustenance. But she contrasts with the wife at least in her 'wifely' role in the lounge room. She can be discreetly chatted-up, within strong, if unarticulated limits. Sometimes her sexuality is frankly a commodity (as in pubs offering 'topless' or 'see-through' barmaids) and in this way contrasts with the ideology of marriage (whatever is said about its reality). Most important, she does not represent the 'civilising' and repressive function of woman as mother, censoring bad language and 'dirty' talk, banning it even in adults from the decorum of the family home. What the pub offers, then, in a schematic, temporary and emotionally uncomplicated form is an alternative version of the dominant familial relationships. Since it is, in effect, a critique of those relationships, it is undoubtedly a threat to them, as has been widely recognised. Although it ostensibly confines that critique to the domain of the pub, the boundaries of domains tend to leak under pressure; and pubs leak more than most.

The conditions of the pub world are implicitly a critique of the dominant ideology of family and suburbia, but this is a male critique from the perspective of male experience. Tim Rowse has commented on an analogous phenomenon in *Australian Liberalism and National Character*. 'The negative image of suburbia', he says, is 'equally a negative image of women':

> A rough equation that seems to be employed is: women, domesticity = spiritual starvation. (Men, wide open spaces, achievement = heroism of the Australian spirit.) The female influence in the culture is often taken to amount to destructive obsession with status and difference. It seems that Lady Macbeth has been written into the myth of mateship. [p. 208]

Women could equally point to their own spiritual starvation in the prison of domesticity, but it would be no advance for both man and woman to face each other in the family lounge room, or the bar of a pub, asking which is the prisoner and which the guard.

We have been describing the basic features of the archetypal pub. In practice, and increasingly as the pub is literally renovated, there are features of pubs that express a relationship of affinity not opposition between home and pub. Pubs are not all equally drab. They can be ranged along a continuum of closeness to or distance from the family lounge—better or worse decor, greater or less comfort—and the less austere and drab they are, the weaker the critique they express of the bourgeois home. There are, as we have indicated, class differences here, so pubs aren't ranged evenly along the continuum, but tend towards one end of the scale or the other. But most pubs have incorporated some features of the home, preeminently the television set. And middle-class houses have incorporated some features of the pub, especially the corner bar and the pool table. This erosion of the boundary between home and pub threatens to make the pub no longer a special privileged place, where antisocial behaviour is sanctioned. Without this boundary the pub no longer has any reason to exist. Or from another point of view, when there is no social need for this alternative pattern of relations and behaviour, the boundary cannot be sustained. This weakened boundary is not only one between cultural domains, but also between genders. As gender roles change in Australian society, so pubs become feminised, homes masculinised; previously masculine work is opened up to women, and masculine leisure is losing its gendered exclusivity.

The mores of the Australian pub are intrinsically related to the inadequacies of sexual relationships in the society as experienced by males, a kind of continuous critique. But it would be wrong not to see the other target of the critique: the workplace. The public bar, as we have said, is significantly often a stopover from work to home. The bare utilitarianism of pub decor has much in common with certain kinds of workplace. Factories, machine shops and warehouses and other working-class places of employment are designed along similar lines. It is as though the setting must be duplicated so that the social relationships can be transformed. David Ireland in his novel *The Glass Canoe* extends this duplication of environment to include noise but notes the crucial difference of human relations:

> I had this job in an office for a while and what the pub noise reminded me of was going down to the factory. As soon as you opened the door the blast hit you. It was everywhere . . . I didn't like that noise, it tried to take you over, leaving no room for anything else. You couldn't think. Unreal, it was. I got out of that job quick.
>
> The noise at the pub was just as loud, but quite different. You could sort of swim in it after a while. By the time you got four or five schooners into you there seemed to be a cushion in your head, anyway. But that's not why I loved to let it wash over me and carry me along. It's because it was people-noise, not machine-noise. What silences there were—not many—were shallow. Like a few inches of water over sandflats. [pp. 2–3]

The factory dehumanises the worker, the pub restores his humanity and his masculinity: in the factory it is the worker who is the commodity, subjected to work discipline and to the boss. In the pub he uses money he has earned to buy drink. There are no bosses and no one to give orders to (except the barmaid). The Australian workplace is organised along gender lines: so largely is the pub (especially working-class pubs). Sexism from the workplace is simply replicated in the pub, and therefore as a critique and a transformation of the workplace the pub is partial and inconsistent, just as it is only partly critical of the home. It sits between the two, uneasy mediator and scapegoat for both. It is interesting to note that it is precisely where it has been most severely criticised—mainly by middle-class critics—that its own critique of dominant relations is most pointed.

There is one obvious limit to the bond of mateship in the Australian pub. Notices, visible or invisible, proclaim 'No Aborigines'. Alcohol and Aborigines have been a problematic issue in Australian life for many years. Until 1964, whites were forbidden to supply them with alcohol, inside or outside pubs, but as with prohibition in the United States this did not achieve full sobriety. Since 1964, supply of alcohol has been legal, and Aborigines have been seen as having a major problem with alcohol. Aboriginal drinking can undoubtedly be destructive of social relations. It is also a response to the damage inflicted on Aboriginal ways of life by innumerable whites, whether drunk or sober. But Aboriginal drinking, like white drinking, obeys its own rules, though sometimes these are different. The tacit domain-based rule for white drinkers is that drunkenness is all right but only in a pub. There is a worrying hiatus between pub and home, focusing on the dangers (and embarrassment) of the drive home. But this rule doesn't work for Aborigines, who do not feel protected by the domain of the pub and who drink in truly public places such as parks. So their drunkenness is more visible and breaks the tacit rule of white drinking; and they get arrested on charges of drunkenness in a vast disproportion to their numbers or even their degree of drunkenness and the danger to the public order they represent. But the punitive treatment of Aboriginal drinkers in public places serves a double ideological function: it separates them off from full participation and membership of white Australian society (they are 'dirty drunks', whereas whites are 'good boozers'), and it vindicates the magic wall around the pub, which both protects white drinkers in their alcoholic anti-society and keeps the subversion and criticism safely within its bounds.

Dionysus Down Under

The defining activity at pubs, of course, is the consumption of alcohol, so the meaning of pubs is bound up with the meaning of alcohol: or, to be more precise, with the structures that assign meaning to alcohol and its different forms. Alcohol, and drunkenness, have a long history in Western culture and a remarkably persistent set of meanings. In the Bible, Noah is associated with the invention of viticulture and wine. His son Ham's crime was to look at his father naked, drunk in his tent (with no one-way glass to protect him). But the best-known wine god is Bacchus, or Dionysus as the Greeks called him. In his *Birth of Tragedy* Nietzsche opposes Greek rationality to Dionysiac rapture, whose closest analogy is physical intoxication in all its forms. The Dionysiac experience, product of Dionysiac ritual, has a political significance:

> Now the slave emerges as a freeman; all the rigid, hostile walls which either necessity or despotism has erected between men are shattered. Now that the gospel of universal harmony is sounded, each individual becomes not only reconciled to his fellow but actually at one with him—as though the veil of Maya had been torn apart and there remained only shreds floating before the vision of mystical oneness. Man now expresses himself through song and dance as the member of a higher community: he has forgotten how to walk, how to speak, and is on the brink of taking wing as he dances.

Dionysiac revellers are depicted (by a later, anti-Dionysiac age) as semi-naked, with pot-bellies—like the archetypal Australian beer-drinker, flushed, demonic and absurd. Nietzsche's conception of the Dionysiac orgy incorporates the radical egalitarian ethos that is also claimed for Australian drinkers in Australian pubs: for 'slave' and 'freeman' substitute 'worker' and 'boss', and you have McGregor's classless hotel bar. There is destruction and violence implicit in Nietzsche's description, a tearing down of rigid walls which may be actual as well as metaphoric, and these walls are aligned with 'despotism', officially sanctioned power, as well as necessity. Add a few broken glasses and jugs, and he could have been at any one of hundreds of Australian pubs on a Friday night.

But Dionysiac orgies were normally constrained and controlled, as far as we know. During a set period, anarchy reigned, social hierarchies were inverted, and the normal rules of everyday life were suspended, on the condition that outside that period, normality would be restored. The world of normality and the Dionysiac anti-world were in functional equilibrium: the pent-up feelings and aspirations of everyday existence were what was expressed in the revelry, and their expression there defused them and allowed the oppressive nature of daily life to continue undisturbed. Or that was the ideal (ideal from the point of view of a ruling class). Violence and drunkenness can't be switched on and off so neatly. But where they continue outside the prescribed time and place, they are easier to police and punish. Where the prescriptions are too precise—as with the six o'clock swill—the repressive system is put under great strain; and a total prohibition can throw the whole apparatus of repression into disrepute, as happened in the United States and as is arguably happening in Australia today over marijuana.

One meaning of drunkenness, then, is radical egalitarianism. But Nietzsche romanticised the experience and failed to include the physical dimension, which is also part of its meaning as well as its effect. The drinkers who have 'forgotten how to walk, how to speak' crash into tables and are lethal at the wheel of a car. As lovers they are unimpressive, and as friends they are unreliable. They are politically fragmented and neutralised, in contradiction to their experience of oneness and power. The political meaning of the pub, and drunkenness, then, has to carry this double message, this intrinsic contradiction.

Alcohol is part of a larger classification system, one that has important cultural meanings and from which we can understand the meaning of specific acts of consumption. Alcohol is both a drink and a drug. The wider system, in Australian culture (which is essentially the same as the system in other Western societies), is as shown over.

In this structure we have left out various 'legal' drugs such as Valium, aspirin, etc.; their place and further classification follow the same general principles. The point to notice about this system is that it is built up by a small number of main principles, and these principles are redolent with cultural meaning. Most of the individual oppositions are homologous, expressing a similar meaning, though with a different inflection. So the choice of aerated waters over milk expresses a similar meaning to a choice of beer over Coca Cola, or spirits over beer, or marijuana over spirits, or heroin over marijuana: danger, risk-taking, pushing at the limits of social conformity, association with the Dionysiac complex. Mixing these components forms a compound meaning which again is consistent

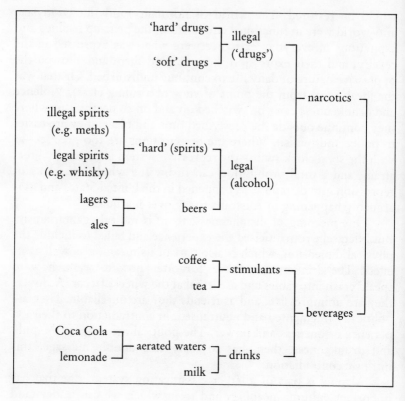

with the scheme. So beer and lemonade (a shandy) has a lower value than, say, rum and Coke, which has a higher value than rum and milk, and so on. In terms of this structure we can see the broad meanings of patterns of consumption and changes in those patterns. Here, for example, is a set of graphs published by the Australian Bureau of Statistics, covering the period from 1938 to 1982.

There are a number of things we can 'read' from these graphs. One is an absence: 'drugs', hard or soft. This of course is partly because there are no official figures on usage, for they are outside the official paradigm—just as alcohol was in the United States under prohibition. So what is presented as a unity under the Nietzschean scheme is treated as fundamentally divided by the meaning-system of the State. But at another level the unity is recognised, even officially, through the existence of 'Drug and Alcohol Centres' and now the National Drug Offensive which treats the human victims of abuse of either or both as having the same essential

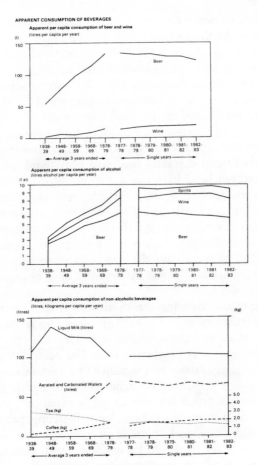

APPARENT CONSUMPTION OF BEVERAGES

Source: Australian Bureau of Statistics

'problem'. There has been, over the past two decades, a radical shift in consumption of drugs, hard and soft, which would show dramatically in any official figures if any reliable ones could be produced.

Since meanings exist as part of a system, meanings about drugs affect meanings about alcohol, and vice versa. The double-think about alcohol produces confusions about drugs, and the fear of drugs infects attitudes to alcohol consumption. In the stereotype of Australian culture, alcohol—purely in the form of beer—figures large, but a fuller reading of the culture must take account of what we can call the Dionysiac complex and the role of drugs in it.

The graph showing the apparent per capita consumption initially confirms the Australian myth of beer as the major Australian alcoholic drink. But the myth also claims a change in recent years, from barbarism to civilisation, marked in two ways: by a shift to civilised social drinking, after the harsh excesses of the six o'clock swill, and by a broadening pattern of drinking, with more wines of ever better quality replacing beer. In this view, wine (especially good wine) signifies European high culture, as against plebeian beer. Per capita, consumption of wine does increase, but not spectacularly and certainly less than beer. And quantities of beer consumed per head have more than doubled in 40 years. It's true that over the five years 1977–83, beer consumption has reached a plateau and even tailed off, and wine consumption has continued to increase slightly, but this leaves the dominant position of beer still unchallenged. This is not a pattern of increasing discrimination and sobriety, but the opposite: essentially the strong survival of patterns laid down many years ago, changed only in superficial ways.

The figures on consumption of alcohol itself, however, challenge the centrality of beer in the Australian Dionysiac complex. The quantity of alcohol consumed in beer is less than that in spirits or wine, and this also is a stable pattern. The centrality of beer in the Australian image, then, is a signifier of a certain equivocation with the Dionysiac impulse. The archetypal Aussie male drinks gallons of beer to get drunk but not to get 'written off', as drinking spirits would do. His preferred beer, lager, is stronger than a Pommie pint of mild, so he marks himself off against that cultural norm, but he does not want to go too far in the other direction. For him beer is a bearer of culture insofar as it is cheap, egalitarian, masculine, social and, when drunk in pubs, significantly differentiated from both home (family/wife) and work (boss). Unlike the archetypal Australian, however, innumerable actual Australians 'graduate', as it's called, to hard drinks, wines and spirits, and knock down various rigid walls in the process of getting themselves totally 'smashed', 'plastered' or 'stoned', to use the common terms (although 'stoned' and 'smashed' are now used to refer to the effects of pot and other drugs).

We will leave alcoholic beverages for the moment and look at the other end of the structure: the figures on milk. Milk is opposed to beer as child to adult, conformity to subversion, safety to danger. In the graph 'Apparent per capita consumption of non-alcoholic beverages', the consumption of milk for many decades neatly counterbalances beer, and in fact outdoes it. Then milk plummets, exactly as the figures for carbonated drinks rise, in the same proportion. It looks like what economists call commodity-substitution, and what a reader of cultures would see as a general shift in patterns of meaning. The spearhead of soft drinks is Coca Cola, containing sugar, as dieticians complain, and also caffein, a drug. So the choice of Coca Cola over lemonade, as well as over milk, signifies in a weak form a first venture away from the safe domesticity of milk, and its success as a product on Australian markets signifies an affirmation of the Dionysiac, carried by all the other trends shown by these figures. In keeping with this, mothers disapprove of their young children drinking Coke in the same terms as they will disapprove of them drinking beer, with the same tacit recognition that it is almost a social obligation. And they will find the same name, 'coke', affectionately used of the illegal Dionysiac substance, cocaine, at the far end of the scale. Common culture and the common language recognise deep affinities between all these commodities, even if the official culture refuses to know.

Youth, Rock'n'roll And The Pub

Although the activities we have described as those of the traditional public bar are by no means the only, or even the majority of, activities that take place in Australian pubs, it is in relation to this classic model that all pub activities define themselves. This is observable in one relatively new use of the Australian pub: as a venue for rock bands. Dating only from the early 1970s the association between the young audiences of rock music, the rock promoters, the bands and the pubs is now a structural feature of the music industry in Australia. It has provided bands with a proliferation of venues, audiences with inexpensive local performances of the music they prefer, and pubs with a mode of access to a young clientele that had previously been relatively alienated from them. The relationship, as we shall see, is not without its contradictions and ambiguities, but it is anything but a shotgun wedding.

The performance of rock music in a pub is an outstanding instance of the Dionysian behaviour outlined in the preceding section. It is a ritual celebration of membership of a group, a group defined by 'the song and the dance'. It is seen to be an expression of the

Pub rock. The Divinyls (photo by Philip Neilsen). Successful as they are, such bands still play the pubs. Christina Amphlett—a parody of male fantasies in her school uniform, garter belts and black stockings, spitting, pouring jugs of water over her head, alternately abusing and seducing her audience—must seem like the 'tiger in the kitchen' gone crazy to the inhabitants of the public bar. For a building to contain performances such as this, as well as the traditional rituals of the public bar, involves real strain. The exuberance of those raging in the lounge bar partly stems from their sense of turning a contradiction into a challenge, locating pub rock permanently on the edge of the delinquent and the uncontrollable.

'natural rebelliousness' of youth, and its experience is participatory, involving the body and the senses. Attending a pub performance is not usually a reflective, Apollonian activity. As American guitarist George Thorogood put it, one night in Sydney's Sundowner, 'this is called rock and roll, not sit and listen'. Rock critics persistently assert its experiential, instinctive, non-rational nature; to understand its special quality, according to one critic, you 'just gotta look . . . and listen . . . and feel'. Like the Dionysiac excess (and, as we shall see, like the surf) it is experienced through the physical senses, not the mind or intellect, and it promotes this physical pleasure as an expression of resistance to the mundane, to the powerlessness of social experience, and thus as a release from oppressive social control. The frequent complaints from the pub's surburban neighbours about the volume of its music are evidence of 'respectable' society's (largely ineffectual) attempts to reassert its right to set the norms of social behaviour. This characteristic alone would make it a potentially threatening force to mainstream rational society, but there is more.

Rock music's form is challenging, aggressive and violent, setting up a central (if often bogus or putative) opposition between its values and those of the rest of straight society. It is capable of rejecting even its own elder statesmen as 'boring old farts' (as the Sex Pistols called the Rolling Stones and The Who) if they fail to maintain an authentically oppositional posture. Its roots as a form and as a social practice are in the group, and its function is largely the ritualised demonstration and celebration of the difference between the group and those outside it. It inevitably takes on subcultural meanings and proposes them to the mainstream culture as challenges, exceptions or propositions for renovation. Its industrial and ideological history is one of a continual, dialectical process of the articulation of opposition to, and incorporation within, the dominant structures of the society.

Rock'n'roll has always been able, however, to establish its specificity as a musical form. A contributing factor is that its musical and lyrical discourses regularly carry connotations of the demonic, the primitive and, in the case of one particularly self-conscious and sardonic band, Kiss, the satanic. Rock music invites, and luxuriates in its ability to generate, fear and loathing—both as an index of its significance as a genuine threat, and as a surrogate for any more explicitly political challenge. This placement of rock'n'roll within the culture, and the nature of its expression in song and dance, causes it to be seen as very much beyond the pale: as a Dionysiac, even nihilistic, force that is irrational, dangerously intoxicating and subversive. Such is the commonly held view of both the music and the audience, and it is a signifier of difference rock'n'roll is proud to wear.

Even though rock'n'roll is a commercial industry, whose most successful performers end up 'crossing over' into the mainstream entertainment industry (we recall the sendups of rock'n'rollers who just want to be 'all-round entertainers'), its special character is derived from its subversive potential. Its history, again, suggests it has the ability to subvert and, simultaneously, produce commercial success regularly if not continuously; the careers of musicians and bands such as Lou Reed, the Doors, the Sex Pistols, even Boy

George, reveal this. In Australia the work of successful bands such as Australian Crawl, Cold Chisel, Midnight Oil or the Divinyls are anything but simple reaffirmations of dominant ways of seeing. So it should not appear odd that an industry such as this should become part of the structure of the pub. The pub, too, offers a release from, and a resistance to, the socially controlled worlds of work and home, while remaining comfortably within and controlled by dominant social values. In this section we trace the connections between the music, the audience and the institution of the pub, to explore this apparent contradiction.

The link between rock'n'roll, youth and the pub has been well documented. Recently *Rolling Stone* published a glossy illustrated guide to Australian rock music called *The Big Australian Rock Book*, edited by rock journalists Ed St John and Paul Gardner. Its attempt to describe the Australianness of Australian rock music appears in two sections: first is an analytical essay that proposes connections and provides a brief history of the 'coming of age' of Australian music; second is an index of the non-rational, instinctive nature of the music in the series of evocative photographs captioned with quotes from musicians about Australian audiences, pubs and the music. The section is titled 'The Music The People The Pubs The Places The Country' in a geometric graphic design that interconnects all elements of the title. The connection between the pubs and the music is a subject of both sections, and the concluding page of the second includes an advertisement, one of only two advertisements in the book, for Jim Beam Whiskey (the other ad is for Roland Synthesisers).

In the essay the terms in which the Australianness of Australian rock music is described are familiar. The same keynotes of independence, innocence, scepticism, egalitarianism and lack of pretension noticeable in most other constructions of Australia we will examine in this book are struck here. Australian rock'n'roll, say the editors, has a 'feistiness, an absence of pretence, a youthful, guileless energy'. It 'reflects a culture which is so consciously egalitarian that success can be as alienating as failure', and 'its denial of artifice... matches its unpretentious, pub origins'. It is seen to articulate an 'Australian view of the world that inspires a mordant, caustic and usually cynical humour'. [p. 8] For a cultural form that is so ready and able to oppose its culture's dominant social constructions, it is noticeably conventional in its representation of itself as a national expression. The traditional function of the pub is endorsed in the articulation of the link between the music and the institution: 'the magic in the music, the music that can set you free, somehow or other got mixed up with the locations where you could set yourself free for a few hours by drinking'. Drink, as the Jim Beam ad indicates, is by no means a coincidental presence in the social activities around Australian rock music, but its releasing and resisting qualities are an intrinsic component of the practices surrounding it, its subject matter and its commercial production.

Drinking contributes to the objectives of the rock audience. When rock fans attend a performance, they want a 'total experience', to 'get off', 'out of control' and definitively 'to rage'. In this, the celebration of the group itself in the packed pub, the alcohol and other stimulants and the music all combine. The Australian 'rage' is signified by specific behaviours, which are noted in *The Big Australian Rock Book* as expressions of difference—both that of the music and that of the audience. The book's quotations deal at length with the subcultural practices of rock audiences in pubs. For example, the British essayist Jan Morris, who has done a number of features for *Rolling Stone* magazine on Australian rock music and its social context, writes:

> The pubs of Sydney are loud with jazz and rock music. Often the thump of it drives the customers into a frenzy, and the bars are full of strapping young Ockers throwing their hands above their heads, whooping and beating their enormous feet. They are not at all like the roisterers of Europe or America, partly because they all seem to be in a condition of exuberant physical well-being, and partly because the tang of their language pervades everything they do. [p. 16]

Here is Dionysus Down Under, with an accent and behaviour all of his own (advisedly), and the word that resonates in the accent is 'rage'. James Reyne, lead singer of Australian Crawl: 'It was what I'd call rage music, very loud and full-on. Smoking bongs, getting drunk, going surfing and generally having a rage; that's what they're into.' [p. 17] Doc Neeson of the Angels: 'the phrase I hear most at gigs in Australia—you hear guys talking at the bar and they are always saying they've come for a rage.' [p. 17] And Peter Garrett of Midnight Oil: 'I think the pub audience want rhythm, and they want it loud. I think they want to be physically involved with it; they see no value in hanging back . . . Australian audiences want to grab a bit of what the band is about and get off on it. In a word, they want to rage. That's the word they use.' [p. 21] It is a word describing immediate sensation, not an investment in the future, and its connotations are those of frustration, resistance and the exploitation of a definitively temporary moment to the limit of its potential. The editors of *The Big Australian Rock Book* are right in seeing this as a way of tasting freedom and in their assumption that the pub provides a mode of release.

The Friday night 'rage' is a youthful transformation of the traditional Friday night with the boys, so it is not surprising that both occur in the domain of the pub. The difference between the two is a difference of age and gender, but not of cultural function. The differences are of degree, not of kind, and probably the most important is the degree to which the interests of the users of the pub conflict with the interests of the wider community. Where the classic bar is becoming a ghetto for its traditional patrons (though still tolerated as an anachronistic mode of using leisure) or is modified in ways that restate traditional values in more acceptable ways (as in the Birdwatchers' Bar), the activities surrounding the performance of a band in a pub are less easily contained within that domain. Rather, they tend to spill out and confront the rest of the society. The social relations between rock fans and the rest are easily polarised, the tolerance quickly withdrawn. Arguments about noise pollution, limits on decibel levels, restrictions on car parking in neighbouring streets, concern about patrons' behaviour on leaving, all indicate the need to continually remind the group of the tension between their values and social control and to preserve precise perimeters within which their behaviour can be contained. There are regular examples of such behaviour getting 'out of control': a pub wrecked by angry patrons in Scarborough; the riot at the Star Hotel in Newcastle; and the most vivid related image, the catastrophic bikie war at the Milperra pub in 1984. The threat to domesticity that is offered by the front bar is one that is still responsive to the restraints of dominant ideology. But rock fans are not as open to such restraints, so the challenge they pose is more criminalised in its depiction (as delinquency) and less subservient to notions of community and responsibility. It is a more volatile and more uneasily mediated grid of conflicts that structure relations between the rock pub and the community than those that structure relations between the pub and the community.

Nevertheless, it is noticeable in *The Big Australian Rock Book* how firmly rooted in dominant images of Australianness the nexus between the pubs, the music, the people, and the country actually is. Firstly, the proposition of a radical egalitarianism in the music and its audiences occurs frequently. In the following instance it survives in references to the lack of pretentiousness, the 'nō-bullshit' attitude of Australian rock audiences:

> Australian audiences have a very low bullshit tolerance; they don't stand for much rubbish. That's what is so healthy about the pub circuit. The people going out to see bands sort them out on that level very quickly, and that's wonderful. There's not much scope for lyrical or musical pretentiousness in Australia. [p. 22]

This is from Iva Davies, who has probably exploited what small scope there is for pretentiousness in Australia better than most, and its usefulness is partly that it reminds us that we are looking at the *representation* of the pub, the music and the audience, not some putative true essence. A lack of pretentiousness is mentioned a number of times in the book and is seen to be equally intrinsic to the pub and the nation and thus naturally reflected in the audiences and the music. It is not the only familiar trait invoked in the analysis:

> There's this fair-go spirit at work with Australian audiences. If people are paying out money they've sweated for, they expect you to sweat in return. Even if they're drunk they know they're being ripped off. [p. 24]
>
> —(Alex Smith, *Moving Pictures*)

Again, a subcultural form is enclosed within the dominant myths. It still represents itself as an oppositional formation, but the values it opposes here are not those of Australian society—it's *expressing* those—but those of the big, capitalist, American, hype-riddled music industry. The difference between the pub-rock subculture and the society at large is mobilised as a metaphor for the opposition between Australian values and those of other western nations. By a metaphorical leap which works not logically but ideologically, the authentic experience of the pub-rocker in opposition to in-authentic suburban gentility is made to bear the meanings of an Australian authenticity that is opposed to the commercialism of America or the gentility of England. Even the six o'clock swill can be mobilised in this way: underlying the following quote from Andy Partridge of the English band XTC are echoes of both the

swill (which he can never have experienced) and of the relative restraint of English pub behaviour (which he clearly has):

> Australian bars I found a little menacing. They're much more
> boisterous than English bars, and then there's the disturbing fact
> that they are tiled as if it were some kind of place where you
> expected a lot of excreta or unwanted mess and they intended to
> swill it down easily with a hose or whatever. I found the fact that
> bars are tiled very intimidating. One night in the Kings Cross
> area of Sydney, I can remember walking past a pub and looking
> in to see it knee-deep in glass. [p. 29]

The final attribute shared by the youth-oriented rock subculture and the pub is their identification with the locality and with
the subculture. Peter Garrett makes the point that the pubs are
the location for the development of bands and their audiences, not
just the site of their performance or commercial exploitation. Most
bands develop from the establishment of an audience in one locality
or group of localities, and their audience constructs a strong identification between it and the pub in which it started. Despite its
enclosure within a very large scale commercial industry, a band's
particular relationship to the pub itself tends to be both personal and
ritualised. As Garrett says, 'every Australian band comes from a
different pub, and it's there they define what they're about. Every
band remembers that pub, and it's more than sentimental value; it's
something much stronger'. [p. 37] The loyalty to the local, the
home away from home, is a sentiment equally familiar to the
regulars in the front bar.

Structurally, the way in which the front bar is a functionalist
reduction of the home is paralleled by the way in which the concert
hall or theatre is proletarianised and reduced in the large lounge
bars that accommodate bands. There is little of the privileging of
performance in the pub, with only a very notional stage area to
separate band from audience, or to offer a sense of the theatrical.
Any theatre that is produced derives from the band itself. The rock-
pub reduces even its 'pub-ness' to its basics: a long bar normally occupies one wall, drinks are served in cans or plastic containers to
avoid breakages, and prices are rounded up to the nearest dollar to
avoid slowing down the transactions with change. Even a comfortable, stylishly decorated lounge can be turned into a rock venue by
extinguishing the atmospheric lights, extending the service area,
removing or concentrating the furniture and, crucially, by simply

admitting twice the number of people the room can comfortably hold. Interestingly, the effect of this overcrowding is not one of claustrophobia, but of the problems caused by having to accommodate so large and so energetic a group. Signs of strain abound in the entry stamps, the bouncers, and the watchful attitude of staff. The effect is to offer the exciting possibility of breaking down the barriers, a sense of the venue being exploded by its contents.

The sense of resistance to containment is made palpable in the rock'n'roll pub. The politics of conflict and control are more ostensibly foregrounded here than has been the case in the public bar since the end of the six o'clock swill, but they are not at all unrelated images. In both cases, the dialectic is one of a contest for control of a domain in which dominant modes of behaviour are subject to attack, and in which the subcultural group struggles to resist the control of the larger culture in order to more accurately express its own interests. In the use of the pub by rock fans, we have a heady image of the strength of that resistance and of the continual imminence of social change.

2   Homes and Gardens

Suburban Homes as Goods to Think with

'It is my opinion, that in the normal development of civilisation, the Decorative Arts are called before all others to manifest the characters of the races.' So wrote Lucien Henry in 1888, in an article that proposed that Australian architects should introduce Australian motifs into their designs wherever possible. He lists Aboriginal images, kangaroos, emus and emu eggs among the motifs worthy of praise. In the early 1960s Robin Boyd's *Australian Ugliness* castigated what he calls 'featurism', the use of decorative, functionless features, as the blight of Australian architecture. Henry's emu eggs never caught on, but if they had, they would have been targets of Boyd's contempt as 'features'.

Henry and Boyd agree, though, in seeing architecture and design as carrying cultural meaning. Of all items of popular culture, Australians spend more money on housing than on any other commodity. Houses, however, are 'goods to think with' (to paraphrase Lévi-Strauss) as well as 'goods to live with', and meaning and function are often indistinguishable in practice. In houses that range in price from $30 000 to $200 000 the basic function of providing shelter is equally well served. It would be conservative to estimate, then, that at least half of the monthly mortgage repayments paid by the average Australian home owner goes towards sustaining meanings, rather than keeping out the rain.

Because most Australian housing is found in the suburbs, it is the meaning of the suburban home we are investigating here. The Australian ideal of owning a home is usually blamed for the creation of the Australian suburban sprawl, but despite attacks from Robin Boyd, Don Dunstan and others, the suburb is not without its defenders; Hugh Stretton, in *Ideas for Australian Cities*, insisted

26

sensibly, if somewhat truculently, that 'you don't have to be a mindless conformist to choose suburban life':

> Most of the best poets and painters and inventors and protestors choose it too. It reconciles access to work and city with private, adaptable, self-expressive living space at home. Plenty of adults love that living space, and subdivide it ingeniously. For children it really has no rivals. [p. 21]

In this last reference to bringing up children, Stretton joins hands with Edna Everage, the doyenne of suburbanites, whose pride in her habitat proclaims the basis for a traditionally Australian myth of superiority: despite fashionable critiques of suburbia, the Australian way is (and always has been) to own a home on a plot of its own, so that the homeless immigrant is magically transformed into a man of property. 'The 'man of property' is a nineteenth-century phrase, and the myth, too, derives from the period. The *Australian Financial Gazette* asserts in 1890: 'Not to have your own home is unpardonable in a country like Australia', and advises that 'the first, the paramount duty of a working man is to acquire a home'. The myth is also invoked in the arguments about rights to land which occurred regularly during the opening of the agricultural leases in pastoral and colonial Australia. The structure of the contemporary suburban Australian home could in fact be seen as a shrunken version of the free selector's dream; the quarter-acre block is a satisfyingly compromised metonym for 'our selection', continuing to assert everyone's right to acquire property in our egalitarian society. This egalitarian principle is also implicit in the relative uniformity of our suburban developments, which do not have to be distinctive to manifest meanings. In this we might see the less acceptable face of egalitarianism; Lucien Henry and Robin Boyd both felt that servility and conformism were two strong messages about the national character transmitted by the Australian housing of their days.

This line of argument leads, however, to the kind of facile Austrophobic attack on suburbia most of us are all too familiar with. Such attacks tend to ignore Stretton's reminder, that most Australians choose to live there. In this book we aim to be more specific, analytic, and revealing than this. To crack the code which will enable us to decipher the meanings of houses and their features so we might gain a deeper understanding of the choices involved, we need

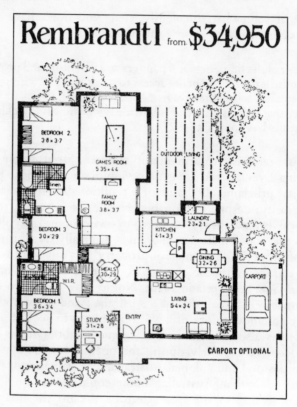

Rembrandt I from $34,950

to start from a sample text: in this case, a display home. To do this, we can place ourselves in the position of prospective buyers visiting such a home, a ritual activity for the weekend that is itself part of popular culture.

Visiting a Display Home

In this instance, the home that has caught our eye is the 'Rembrandt', priced from $34 950, by Artisan Homes. The price promises a wealth of meanings but it is a 'budget' home and still within reach of the average family who might wish to devote a substantial proportion of their income towards appropriating to themselves the meanings embodied in that property. The name itself is nicely calculated: the house's title alludes to high art and therefore dispenses notions of excellence and high status, but the implicit elitism is slightly defused by the builder's name, Artisan Homes, in which the more craftsman-like, proletarian connotations dominate. As prospective buyers, after all, we are on a budget and do not want to aim too high and offend egalitarian ethics—but nor would we want to buy inferior work. As advertised, the 'Rembrandt' by Artisan offers a compromise between the hint of upward mobility and the down-to-earth rejection of elitist pretension. If the account so far seems somewhat patronising, it is worth remembering that there are plenty of cultures where this opposition goes totally unrecognised and the elitism is openly and unashamedly displayed. The negotiation aided by the advertisement for the 'Rembrandt' is relatively subtle, since it enables a deeply contradictory series of myths and ethics (primarily those of the elitism of wealth and the levelling principle of egalitarianism) to be resolved in ways that satisfy all parties.

We start our 'reading' as we get out of the car, and in order to perform this reading we need to use two pairs of oppositions that are deeply structured into many aspects of Australian culture, and into this house in particular. The first, and most important, is that between nature and culture. Australians have always had contradictory ideas about this relationship. Nature is at one and the same time harsh, unforgiving and anti-human, but also refreshing, true and where the urbanised Australian finds his or her 'true' self. The suburbs reflect this contradiction as home builders and owners combine signs of both, enabling them to come to a point of balance where the threat inherent in all contradictions is temporarily defused. The other opposition is concerned with a way of making sense of culture; it is the opposition between the private and the public, between the individual and society. The meanings that we make are both meanings for ourselves and meanings for others, and our houses are both shelter and sense for us, and statements about us to others. This gives the public some rights over 'our' property and inevitably sets up some contradictory impulses as we choose, plan, furnish and decorate our homes.

Let us look first at how this house copes with the relationship between nature and culture. We note the small, well-kept front lawn, with a few 'natives'. The house is unequivocally 'culture': the lawn is equivocally 'nature'—it is growing, it is not concrete, but compared to the native shrubs around it is felt as less than natural. What Boyd noted as 'arborophobia', fear of trees, is less endemic in

Australian suburbs now; while builders may still raze all trees on the block, house owners now tend to replant with natives which are both natural and controlled. But the opposition to the Australian version of nature which dominates the history of Australian architectural styles is created by a number of factors, not least among them the initial yearning for the landscapes of old England which mark early pictorial representations of the landscape and early attempts at horticulture in the colonies. The gradual infiltration of native plants into our suburban gardens, and the corresponding withdrawal of European-styled gardens, suggests that a process of legitimation is being acted out that mirrors positive changes in the Australian's relation with the landscape. Certainly the low-maintenance factor recommends the native garden to the house-proud, but that recovery of leisure—the delivery from the garden's tyrannical domination of the weekend—also signifies a growing sense of accommodation with the land, through which culture and nature have been made to coexist more harmoniously. While creative and adaptive, the highly stylised character of the version of 'nature' found in the native garden is nevertheless controlled by an edging of old railway sleepers and a covering of woodchips, the latter suggesting how ambiguous the putatively harmonious relationship can be.

There is no fence around 'Rembrandt'. This is unsurprising, since this home is offered for inspection by the public. But the absence of fences is a common feature in such houses in use, in most of our newer suburbs. This has not been true at all times in all suburban Australia, and derives from American influences. It may seem to signify a new openness to society, an easy relaxed abolition of the boundary between individual and society. It is, however, more equivocal than that. The manicured lawn is both flat—so that eyes can pass easily over it—and smooth—so that feet will not presume to. No signpost is needed to say 'Don't walk on the grass', because the path signifies 'walk here'. The front garden is normally set out to be seen to its best advantage from the street. Typically, no one in the house makes constant use of the rooms that look out on to the front, or not during daylight hours. The front garden, then, consists of meanings *for* the public, for society, though one of these meanings is that the house itself is private property. The message of this display home is at one extreme, in that the rights of the owners are understated, the rights of the public overstated, because the people trooping through it are primarily members of the public and only potentially the exclusive owners of this desirable residence. At the other extreme would be large gates and a long path winding through thick foliage to an obscured front door; wealth is frequently spent in Australia to purchase privacy—economics, exclusivity and elitism go together here, as in other areas of the culture.

The 'codes' operating here may offer everyone a range of possible meanings, but the full range isn't equally available to everyone. It costs money to afford lavish privacy; to give the public a display and yet withhold from them the essential property. There is also another constraint on freedom of expression. The messages we are examining are messages about social relationships. Overt declarations of hostility are frowned on and effectively controlled, except among the very wealthy who are allowed to have large gates, high walls, and even guards. But even these were not enough for one Perth millionaire who had to raise his garden walls because coach tour operators were treating his house as a tourist attraction. The public's right to look, to share possession by looking, is the corollary of the owner's responsibility to display a public front. Property that is hidden from public view fails to conform to the values of the suburban community: it is a message without a reader, an owner talking to himself (a sure sign of social deviance) or to his close friends (an equally sure one of elitism). Secrecy is the sign of elitism, the mark of a 'tall poppy' that requires the egalitarian public to cut it down. This attitude was exploited in one story in The *Western Mail* (9 October 1982) in which the newspaper joined with its readers in the public duty of attacking such antisocial secrecy: it identified the best vantage point from which to view a newly erected millionaire's house. The house may be 'remote from neighbours and difficult to approach by road', and the owner may have paid $5.5 million for the block, but nothing can keep it from the proprietorial, egalitarian gaze of those readers 'prepared to risk a change in tides'. Mere money can't get you away from the rest of us, mate, the *Western Mail* (owned by the extremely rich and very private Robert Holmes à Court) says on behalf of its readers.

These conventions of the public and the private are organised by an ideology of fundamental community, where the individual is subordinated to a society containing no antagonistic elements: these mark differences of wealth, perhaps, but no class conflict, hardly even a criminal element. One can see the very conformity and predictability of houses in our suburbs as actively and explicitly repressing hierarchical class distinctions. The clearest example of

Suburban Brisbane. Although many of the newer suburbs in outer Brisbane are indistinguishable from their counterparts in any Australian city, the high-set, verandahed, timber 'Queenslander' is unique. It is subject to extensive modifications, however. In this picture we can see at least three. The far house preserves its original state, with open verandah and downstairs area. The middle house has the verandah closed in and a garage built downstairs, thus attacking the virtues of the open shaded spaces in order to create more space for the family. The house in the foreground has taken on the discourses of the suburbs of the 1950s with its brick veneer, aluminium shades, English-style garden and wrought-iron balustrade.

this is seen in just the area of housing where such distinctions might be most invidious: Housing Commission developments. Here the variation on the double-fronted bungalow (with porch, without porch, porch on left, porch on right) is mechanical, symmetrical and meaningless; each difference is sufficient to distinguish one house from the next but minimal enough not to infer differences of status. The egalitarian ethic still retains its vigour, so that looking for something too different or too much 'better' can be interpreted as perverse, snobbish or unAustralian.

The ideology of fundamental community creates an image of society in which gratuitous differences are represented as dangerous. Changes in design trends in suburban housing, consequently, tend to be large scale. So, in our sample display home, the use of exposed beams, highlighted brickwork, interior arches and pseudo-

Spanish effects are part of a massive trend away from the brick, the concrete porches, and the wrought-iron balustrades of the 1950s. The dominance of natural brick over paint and cement rendering, the use of natural or unfinished woodwork, and the utilisation of outdoor areas, all continue the search for a balance between nature and culture which seems to provoke so many of the design features in the contemporary suburban home. In the northeast, 'the Queenslander', a high-set verandahed wooden house, is subject to fewer inflections, perhaps because it has always seemed so definitive a solution to its own local problems. In other states the more gratuitous touches—the full-blown Spanish treatment, the Greek pillars on the verandah, or the use of an atrium as a central feature—provide elements of exotica which are signs of the Mediterranean origins of many Australians. This mix between English and Mediterranean influences brings a vitality and a controlled unthreatening clash of cultures to suburban buildings in the same way that it does to society as a whole. Our 'Rembrandt', however, modestly uses the hidden entry in its double front as its main distinguishing characteristic. This itself denotes privacy and is related to the use of walls, long drives, and so on, employed by the very rich. It does not signify great wealth, but rather a wish to have more cheaply what wealth can provide in abundance, and it makes one very sensitive to the differentiations signalled within the house that mark out private and public areas.

The route we follow to enter the 'Rembrandt' is somewhat circuitous. We come down the right side of the house, turn left, then reach the porch, turn right and enter. Here we are faced with a choice: left, right or straight ahead. To the left is the study and main bedroom—the most private area of the house. Even as viewers we don't turn left, so strong are the signals sent by the placing of walls and doorways. Straight ahead (with a further turn to the left) would be the family rooms—more private, but not forbidden. To the right, following the natural curve initiated by our entrance is the 'living room'. The freedom we have as viewers to go anywhere in this house, which might become our own, allows us to appreciate the strength and subtlety of the categories that have been set up to influence the behaviour of visitors of different kinds. The three directions in practice classify three different kinds of person: non-family (to the right), family (straight ahead) and marital couple (left). These three meaings can be signified by different signifiers in other styles of housing. In two-storeyed houses, upstairs/downstairs signifies private/public. Where there is a verandah this carries some of the meanings of outer as public. These different signals are themselves significant differences in status and social attitude, part of a system that is capable of producing an infinity of shades of meaning around a common core.

The long circuitous route to the right, into a living room displaying expensive and tasteful prints, plushly upholstered furniture and knick-knacks is in effect the same kind of ambiguous frontier as was the front garden. Where the front garden offers the wealth of nature gratis to the public, the living room offers the wealth of culture; but while the function is the same, in the living room the claim is more strongly made that these features are the property of the owner, and their meanings are more specifically individualised. This is where the 'featurism' that offended Robin Boyd is still most rampant. Boyd disliked the insistent individualism of featurism, but this is not an accident: it is its primary meaning, carried in order to qualify some of the meanings borne by the house's exterior. The choice of decoration and furnishing in the suburban living room is the means available to the individual to express her or his individuality within the demands of society. The influence of the social can be seen in the overall 'style'—furnishings, carpets and curtains are, after all, purchased from stores whose goods are designed to sell to a mass market and which therefore share common features of style. But within this style there is scope for the exercise of taste, and, as we argue in Chapter 5, taste, as a personal use of style, is where individuality is expressed within the social. One only needs to look at the catalogues of furniture stores, at the samples of carpets, curtains and wallpapers to realise the immensity of the scope for combinations of personal choices that is offered within the conformity of a social style. So, too, one has only to look at the shelves of gift shops to see the same phenomenon in ornaments.

The style of the living room again reflects the multicultural nature of Australian society. There are specialist furniture stores that import Italian furniture, and the ornaments available in gift shops show a wide range of ethnic origins—English, Mediterranean, Aboriginal, Asian. Traditional middle-class taste, with its preference for homogeneity and understatement, often finds the vitality, variety and brightness of many Australian living rooms 'tasteless'. In fact, the word betrays its origin; it is merely saying that the 'tasteful' middle classes, usually with English origins or aspirations, exclude any other styles from the realm of 'taste'. What they would call 'vulgarity' can equally well be seen as vitality, variety and self-confidence, characteristics that should not be undervalued in Australian society. In this we again see how what is the distinctively Australian has a working-class inflection that is opposed to middle-class restraint and is thus devalued by middle-class standards of taste: it lacks 'style'. So middle-class designers and trendsetters work against this 'stylelessness' (which of course is nothing of the sort: such styles are strongly marked and significant; what they lack is middle-class 'taste'). This consistent attempt to mobilise upward aspirations in many Australians is not only a movement towards the establishment of a particular middle-class taste as the 'natural' style for the suburban home, it is also a movement away from the varied ethnic origins of Australian society towards an Anglo-centric homogeneity.

If we look carefully at the floor plan of the 'Rembrandt' we can see how comprehensively the organisation of the house expresses key features of the ideology of the family. It expresses social relationships—different categories for family and friends, and for the married couple and their children—yet it also blurs their boundaries. The kitchen is an 'open' kitchen, with no walls dividing it from the rest of the living area; but the structure of benches and cupboards still corrals the mother into the command centre of the house. The opening of the kitchen does not free the mother from the role of cook, but it does signal a change in the meaning of that role in family and social life. The kitchen used to be hidden from the dining room: from it would emerge, almost miraculously, the food for family and guests. This is a residue of the time and class when cooking was seen as a menial task to be performed by servants and then by the mother-as-servant. As she brought the meal to the table, her servant role was left in the kitchen and she became mother-wife or hostess as she sat at the table. Now, however, cooking is seen as less menial, more creative, so not only is the mother-cook not to be excluded from activity and conversation in the living or dining areas of the house, but her role as cook is given a highly visible centrality. The placing of the kitchen between the family meals area and the visitors' dining area, and its openness, establishes the woman as the mediator between the family and the guests, and suggests that children only have access to the visitors and to the 'dining area' through the mother's grace. The laundry, opening off the kitchen, is effectively made invisible to the guest, convenient for the woman in the kitchen, and a long way from the man's private place, the study. Its invisibility suggests that the work performed there is menial, not creative or positive. The washerwoman has not shared the cook's move up the ladder of social acceptability and into public visibility.

Just as the man is excluded (or rather insulated) from the laundry, the children are excluded from the master bathroom—through the interposition of a study on one side and an ensuite bathroom/toilet on the other. Lower down the market will be a house with a semi-ensuite: a bathroom/toilet with two doors, one from the main bedroom, the other from the rest of the house (which otherwise would be without one). The double door is a contradiction in this room, which should be both buffer and inner sanctum. An even more up-market house will have even more barriers between the married couple and the rest of their family. The equivocations with the complex relationships *within* the so-called nuclear family are expressed in innumerable, often quite expensive, sets of signs. These then become 'desirable' features of the house, a social set of signifiers expressing very immediately and directly the problems of social relations that generate them. As we look at the ensuite bathroom/toilet in this 'Rembrandt' house, however, we note that it is not the presence or absence of it alone that is socially significant. The 'Rembrandt II' ($25 950) has a semi-ensuite. That doesn't mean the family that lives in it is differently structured. It might just be that they cannot afford the extra $9000, for as we saw earlier, wealth is frequently used to purchase privacy, with its connotations of exclusivity and elitism. It is unsurprising that this should be apparent inside the house, as well as outside.

The Ideal Home

There are some important similarities between a tour around a display home and the perusal of the kind of glossy magazine that is devoted to displaying 'ideal' homes. In both, a private space is offered to the public gaze. The house is offered as a commodity and a showcase for other commodities. But there are some differences, of degree if not of kind. A house like the 'Rembrandt' would never make it to the pages of *Home and Living* or *Belle*, and the people who troop through it on a Sunday afternoon would not be admitted into the prestigious homes of the glamorous trendsetters who dominate such magazines.

In these magazines, class boundaries are dissolved, as readers are treated as appreciative and honoured guests. Yet this guest is somewhat anomalous, too; a mixture of friend and stranger, allowed into intimate spaces such as bedroom, bathroom and kitchen, but informed, like a stranger, about the history of ornaments and pictures and given authoritative judgments on the taste of the designer/furnisher (who may or may not be the owner).

One of the insistent meanings of such ideal homes is class. Social status is proven by the range and quality of possessions, whose costliness is proof of 'taste'. Yet everything is ordered for display, for use by the spectator not by the owners. In a house that is 'lived in', lower down the market, vulgar display is joy for the owner, expressing meanings for the self—perhaps reminders of happy times, individual people and places who are known and loved. Good taste, in contrast, pleases and impresses the eye of the visitor. Style leaves nothing to accident. All colours are coordinated, each object complements or contrasts with others, and all rooms feature a feature.

In the extracts from glossy magazines reproduced below, we see something of what is valued and given value by such representations. The pictures show a house emptied of people, host and hostess, family and guests alike. The house is not the domain of domestic labour, it has become a work of art. The labour, signified only through its products, is creative, elegant and, above all, finished. As Rosalind Coward has pointed out in *Female Desire*, where she deals with the same subject from a British perspective, the labour signified in such houses is the opposite of the normal domestic work carried out mostly by women—work that is a repetitive 'struggle against things and mess'. It is an image, not of 'light and airy living' but of a bright absence of life, an elimination of other people with their inconsistently competing claims, energies and values. And the unreality of this image, far from detracting from its appeal, is its essence.

Yet it is not simply unreal, unrelated to tendencies to be seen in more ordinary homes and situations. These homes are offered as machines for facilitating one function, entertainment, and this function has an important role in the economy of labour in the home. In the traditional division of labour in the house along gender lines, entertainment transforms the labour of the woman from unseen servant to presiding presence. It marks a moment when the constant round of cooking and providing is momentarily fractured.

Light and airy living

The master bedroom is simple but stylish. An antique dressing table complements the black cane bedhead. The fabric covering the bedside table matches the pink dotted bed linen.

The drawing room enjoys the breathtaking view by day and night. Gold chintz covered sofas blend harmoniously with the cigar coloured walls, the Regency table with brass inlay has drop sides.

The colour scheme in the sitting room and throughout the house is subtly understated; monochromatic shades of terracotta harmonise with the soft colour of the limestone.

This fabulous bathroom features a stained glass window and black slate wet area. Brass taps and shower screen frame contrast strikingly against the black.

The formal lounge, elegant, features mushroom cushion-covered sofas and glass coffee table. Selected adorn the walls and a lam Queen Anne-style corne warm glow.

The family room is divided into distinc areas by the careful placement of the furniture; is overlooked by the kitchen and leads to the garden courtyard. Perfect for the owners who enjoy informality and love to entertain.

Visual and **verbal** representations of the ideal home.

Normally the domestic routine is a cyclic process, with no end point and no pause that allows its products to be recognised and valued: cooking, eating, washing up, shopping, cooking, eating. . . Entertaining provides such a point of public recognition. The role of 'hostess' has connotations of status and power that 'housewife' does not. One function of these glossy magazines, then, is to offer a revaluation of domestic labour, reshaping the social world so that the house, the domain of the private, is at its centre, an effortless source of prestige and appreciation to woman as queen. As such, it implicitly expresses dissatisfaction with the dominant gender roles while making them for a moment seem rewarding and acceptable. But in this package, critique is not evenly balanced with legitimation. On the contrary, the critique is only acknowledged as far as it is to make the legitimation more convincing, and its tendency is probably towards making women more content with their unapplauded domesticity.

Running through the montage of quotations from glossy magazines reproduced here, we see three themes that recur. One is the resolution of contradictions; see the repetitions of 'harmonious', or the use of words such as 'match', 'blend' and 'complement', or the yoking of opposites by 'but' and 'yet' (e.g. 'cosy yet elegant', 'simple but stylish'). Given the inverse relationship between ideological images and material conditions we can assume that this repetition of harmony expresses a sense of the difficulty of achieving it in everyday life. The tension concerns the claims of public and private. The public is the realm where the owner amazes and impresses the onlooker, with 'breathtaking views' or 'striking contrasts' or markers of tradition ('Regency table', 'Queen Anne-style corner table', 'antique dressing table'). The other major signifier is intimacy. Discreet hints of sexuality are present even in public rooms and public duties, conveyed through the key words 'enjoy' (even the drawing room is turned on by the view provided for its gratification) and 'warm' (with a table lamp atop the Queen Anne-style table cheekily reminding the world that there's more to domestic bliss than endless entertainment).

Although most of the work of these glossy magazines goes into glamorising and sustaining traditional gender roles, they also reveal signs of real shifts away from those roles. Here the form of the Australian kitchen, in magazines and in reality, is an important indicator of one shift, a redefinition of cooking as no longer exclusively 'woman's work'. Advertisements for kitchens and their applicances are increasingly showing Dad in the kitchen. House design is carrying similar messages. 'The kitchen is designed for whoever is working there' (Webb and Brown-Neaves pamphlet), 'the kitchen is designed for the creative chef' (*West Australian*, 10 October 1984), 'Designed to human engineering principles' (Webb and Brown-Neaves pamphlet). High tech has come into the kitchen, reconstituting in the process the conventional gender signifiers and gender roles. In the ideal kitchen shown in the photograph above, we see the typical forms of the contemporary Australian kitchen: rectangular functional shapes, gleaming white surfaces, and costly and efficient labour-saving machines. There is no attempt to imply that this is the 'warm' cosy heart of the house where the woman can labour, happily assured that somehow she will be rewarded by giving and receiving love.

If we stayed with this level of analysis, accepting the ideological schemes these glossy magazines try to impose, it would be hard to see the magazines in any positive sense as evidence of a vital Australian popular culture. The world they represent is neither popular nor very Australian. Magazines produced in Australia, such as *Belle* or *Homes and Living*, are displayed by newsagents alongside magazines produced in Britain or the United States, and it is difficult to distinguish the country of origin from format alone. 'Australianness' does occasionally occur as a signifier, but most of the illustrations in Australian magazines could have appeared in other international magazines. The photographs of the lounge and kitchen, shown above, are typical in this respect. If the locale of a home is identified as Australian, the effect is not to give an Australian inflection to the international style but, on the contrary, show yet another Australian whose house speaks 'internationalese' with impeccable correctness. These magazines remove Australianness from their ideal realm, along with other signifiers of vulgarity and low caste.

There are some exceptions to this generalisation. In Australian magazines the products advertised can be purchased in Australia, at the outlets nominated. Australian readers are addressed as potential consumers who can do something about it, whereas the images found in non-Australian magazines are further out of reach. Some Australian magazines, at the lower end of the market, provide a specific information service to consumers that requires local knowledge (e.g. *Home Project Kits—Australia*), and these magazines have no outside competitors. Such differences, slight though they may seem on the surface, point to the real difference that brings these magazines within the domain of Australian popular culture. Speaking to Australian readers of these magazines we learned of some of the uses they made of them, which were not always along the lines an ideological reading would suggest. For these women the images were not illusions whose insidious power left them helpless victims of the bourgeois gender trap. They used them as 'goods to think with', as a source of ideas and meanings to build into their own houses and lifestyles. They did not see this as an attempt to ape their betters, in a way that simply confirmed the superiority of the superior and consolidated male supremacy and female servitude. On the contrary, these meanings became available to the women to enable a creative working over of the conditions of their material existence, renegotiating gender roles and constructing new identities for individuals within the family. Such recycling of the elements of mass-circulated culture is a creative use of the imagination and a clear example of the power of the subordinate to make their own popular culture out of the most unpromising materials. As in so many instances, the Australian accent is to be found not in the texts themselves, where capitalism seems to hold unchallenged sway, but in the uses made of those texts as they are incorporated into the structures of everyday life.

Outdoor Living

It is time now to return to our tour of the 'Rembrandt'. From the house we step outside, into the 'outdoor living' area. This is possibly the most ritualised of spaces in our homes, dominated by codes of behaviour and gradually being converted with technology into a place of real complexity. The Australian male has turned the outdoor living area into an expensive and central feature of the suburban home. Here Ted Bullpit reigns, surrounded by his range of insect sprays, barbecue 'tools', lighting fixtures, garden furniture and plants in a variety of rustic pots. In a 'Rembrandt'-style home, typically, the outdoor living area is semi-covered, paved, with a table and chairs. Here nature and culture are brought into a different balance—the covering reflecting distrust of the weather, the tables and chairs indicating a comfortable assurance of its docility.

At one end of the outdoor living area is a space to be filled by a barbecue, the high altar in the ritual of outdoor living that signifies more than any other single item. Cooking is, as the anthropologist Claude Lévi-Strauss has shown us, one of the basic means by which nature is transformed into culture in all societies. In *The Raw and The Cooked*, Lévi-Strauss explains that raw food, especially meat, is raw nature and as such cannot be accepted into culture without undergoing the transformation of cooking. Only animals eat raw meat. But the elaborate rituals of preparing a dinner party, which turn food into the most markedly cultural product, are reserved for the formal indoor dining area. Midway on this scale of culturising nature by cooking is the less-formal family meals area. Here the meal will be less elaborate, and the food will have been subject to fewer cultural processes in its cooking and will consequently be a step or two nearer to nature. Some of the food eaten here may well be 'convenience food'—that is, food that has been partly or wholly cooked by an industrial processor instead of the housewife. This does not invalidate our reading, for after all the food manufacturers constantly assure us how natural their product is and how little their processing has transformed it from its natural state! The barbecue is the most 'natural' way of cooking: culture is closest to nature here. There are no utensils intervening in the process, a minimum of fats and oils, just the natural elements of fire and meat. There is a significant reversal of sex roles in barbecue cooking that may only be explicable in terms of this nature–culture relationship. Outdoor cooking is typically performed by the male, seeking an analogy for his definitively masculine role as hunter in 'natural' societies. The hunter male proudly cooks the meat which he has symbolically caught and, in the barbecue enactment of 'natural' social relations, brings it to the salad which his wife (the gatherer or cultivator) has prepared indoors in the sphere of culture. The barbecue meal celebrates the transformation of nature into culture.

Even the colloquial spellings, Bar BQ, BAR-B-QUE, or BBQ, are signs of the attempt to leave culture indoors, in this case the culture as the socially accepted 'correct' use of language. The phonetic 'Bar BQ' seems a more 'natural' way of transferring speech on to paper than does the correct spelling. Speech is, after all, the more natural form of language, writing the more cultured, so the more closely that writing approximates to speech the more natural it appears to be.

A revealing marker of a shift in Australian attitudes to the nature–culture opposition is the fate of the traditional verandah. The verandah is still common in the country and is still found in colonial houses currently being gentrified in our cities' inner suburbs. In Queensland its use is crucial in the height of summer during the regular afternoon storms, when the cooler air of the verandah is preferable to the oppressive heat of the house. In many ways it signifies an ideal balance between nature and culture, while also collapsing the private–public opposition by turning the outdoors front verandah into a living and entertaining area. Yet most older verandahed houses in Brisbane and other cities have been converted—the verandah closed in to become another bedroom or to extend living space inside. There is also a countertrend, so that many are now being restored and opened up, but the resolution offered by the verandah seems to be rejected as a norm, and a sharper vision of this opposition between indoor–outdoor reasserted.

This taming of nature into culture must be sympathetically and tactfully done. It cannot be too crude and obvious, or culture will lose the kudos of appearing natural. The ritual of the Bar BQ is as formal and culture-created as a high church mass, yet its appeal is its apparent informality and naturalness. It is the ritual equivalent of the native garden, culturally controlled, cultivated nature in which the significance of nature is foregrounded over that of culture. The opposites of nature and culture are brought into a similar relationship in the ubiquitous phrase 'outdoor living', where 'outdoors' refers to nature and 'living' to culture. The phrase sets up a contrast between itself and the (indoor) living room.

Both are for purposes of entertainment, but one is formal (decorous, guarded, public, distant), the other is informal (relaxed, relatively close). It is outside the house, but the house acts as a buffer between this space and the rest of the community. The outdoor living space signifies an opposite valuation of the meaning of 'property'. The general meaning of property is that it *enables* privacy (so the master bedroom is the most proprietorially possessed of all the rooms of the house). But the 'outdoor living' area expresses a repudiation of that whole ideology. Inside, indoors equals constraint, materiality, while outside nature signifies freedom, relaxed, harmonious relationships. It carries a counter-ideology that is a critique of the ideology of possession, the ideology of suburbia.

The counter-ideology affirming nature over culture is one of the enduring myths of Australia, signifying a distinctive Australian relationship with the landscape. The openness and friendliness of the Australian people is linked with the outdoors as the natural location for social interaction, and this in turn connects with the

'Suburban' Aborigines. Sir Russell Drysdale constructing the outback for suburbia. 'Mullaloonah Tank' is a typically popular picture in Australian suburban homes, even in Western Australia, where a state election in 1986 showed both major parties equally eager to repudiate land rights for Aborigines. The Aborigines are painted in the same colours as the desert, at one with it. But these are not noble savages—they wear cast-off white clothing and stand erect beside a primitive and obviously inadequate shelter. Drysdale has used a restricted colour range, mainly reds, browns and yellows, a decorative parody of the Land Rights flag, and reminiscent of the palette of traditional Aboriginal art. In many ways this painting confronts white suburbia with its threatening other. But not too much. This is a print, a copy of a picture of reality, enclosed in a frame which cost many times as much as the print itself, like a view from a train window. This print is likely to hang on the wall of the formal dining area (not in the family room), where it will add decorative interest to that rarely used space. Certainly it will not provoke discourse about Aboriginal health, housing or land rights. Context and conventions neutralise the force of the content, they are a way of 'cooking' the outback and the Aboriginal problem, making the rawness of it (too) easily digestible. (*Collection—The Art Gallery of South Australia, Adelaide*)

kind of existence mythologised in the swagman, the itinerant bush worker, or the archetypal Australian brewing tea over a campfire. The outdoors of the suburban home acts as a compressed signifier for this image of Australian existence, renovating our irrevocable urbanism by overlaying it with a sense of harmony with nature, of being at ease in, and preferring, the outdoor environment to the constraints of the home. Even the particular varieties of materialism we go in for can be seen to have meanings in this area: the yacht in the driveway of some 'Rembrandt' homes, the beach shack which may be a second home, the campervan, the four-wheel drive, to mention some more expensive commodities, or the use of exposed timber, exposed brickwork, or prints of Russell Drysdale's paintings of the outback or Aborigines, to mention a few less structural signifiers. The outdoor living area of the 'Rembrandt', then, seems to directly contradict the meanings we find in the interior of the home, suggesting a deep ideological division within the ways in which the Australian will use the home. The suburban home is not as simple, nor as banal, as it looks to many observers.

But, as with the openness we looked at earlier, such meanings must be set in context. The meaning of a cultural form is a structure, not an item. In the structure that is the typical suburban home, the primary meanings are carried by the dominant functional elements. With the other meanings we have looked at, the 'features' carry not only their meanings, but also their status as subordinate meanings—as qualifications of dominant meanings or as statements of the individual within social conformity. To have a Drysdale picture of Aborigines in the outback on your living room wall signifies an awareness of another order of existence in opposition to comfortable suburbia, but the weighting between the two worlds is not equal. The primary commitment is clearly to the values of white suburbia. Boyd's criticism of 'featurism' is, we can suggest, exactly wrong in one important respect. He objected to the features being added to basic structures and obscuring the meaning of those basic structures. It may be that the 'features' typically express a critique of dominant structures and dominant meanings, and that what is wrong, if anything, is only that this critique is typically partial, fragmentary and unconvinced. So, if the outdoor barbecue implies a critique of suburban constraints, it may not go far enough in suggesting alternative social structures. Instead of removing features from the house, a radical architecture might try to create a house out of the meanings carried by the features—the critiques, the compensatory ideologies that exist to oppose the dominant ideology.

But that is to ask for radical architecture, not popular culture. What we have in Australian suburban architecture is something more interesting: a set of texts from which can be read both ideological forms and various kinds of resistance to those forms. Houses are not commonly built by their owners, they are merely consumed (bought, lived in, 'improved') by them, but as a mass medium housing is more directly responsive to the intentions and meanings of its users than is the case with most other mass media and forms of popular culture. As Lucien Henry said, housing styles 'manifest the character' of a race (or nation, or social class) with special force and transparency. The money spent on this class of meanings cannot be without significance, in Australia as elsewhere.

The Old Backyard

Our analysis of the text of the 'Rembrandt' house doesn't presume that all contemporary houses in Australia are really more or less like it. On the contrary, the unity is primarily to be found in the underlying code, which is in fact a system for producing significant differences. These may be differences between different regions or communities and different levels of social status or aspiration, or they may include differences that are more localised and individual. But there will be one thing common to this whole range: the meaning of contemporaneity. Scattered amongst all the 'contemporary' houses are houses from previous periods, which acquire a new and powerful meaning from the juxtaposition. They come to signify the past. Far from being irrelevant to the meaning of contemporary styles, they are indispensible to it. We have seen the continual process of allusion and quotation by which contemporary houses create a version of history, but houses that are actually old do the same with far greater persuasiveness—though they are not immutable either, and can be restored in various ways that are themselves a kind of rewriting of history. 'How things were' lives on as a myth of a vanished golden age or as a baseline that confirms the superiority of the present. Either way, features of contemporary housing form a system of oppositions with houses of the past, a set of transformations whose meaning is part of Australian cultural history.

There have undoubtedly been some significant changes in Australian suburban homes during the past 30 years, changes that everyone recognises and accepts as significant. As a start towards defining this change we will take one development: the transition from what used to be called the 'backyard', and is now more usually termed the 'outdoor living area'. Examples of 1950s-style backyards still survive, but these don't exhaust the semiotic effects of this feature on the present. Many Australians still remember the backyards of their youth or hear their parents speak warmly about them. These memories shouldn't simply be dismissed as nostalgia for a vanished past. It's true that these memories are not entirely reliable, but they are not total fictions either. The memories and the discourses which carry them are facts of the present, and the shifts they have undergone are not random or unmotivated. The 1950s house with its backyard occupies a semiotic space determined by both past and present, and we can't leave it out of any comprehensive account of contemporary suburbia.

The 'backyard' of the 1950s contrasted with the outdoor living area of today in a whole set of features. Unlike the pergola-ed, well-shaded, and partially paved object of today, the backyard had few concessions to 'outdoor living'. It may have had one shady tree, perhaps bearing a homemade swing or the marks of frequent climbing. This tree, often as not, would stand in splendid isolation in the grassy patch in the middle of the yard which was called a lawn only when it had to be mowed. Even this single tree was under threat if its shade challenged the sphere of influence of the other dominant feature: the Hills Hoist for drying the clothes. If there was a garden in the backyard it was usually constituted by choice from among three main elements: the flowering bushes around the back entry or the outside toilet, the bordering bushes or shrubs around the paling fence perimeter, and the vegetable plot which served the practical rather than ecological purpose of providing fresh vegetables cheaply for the family. Any possibility of the backyard providing a display for visitors was denied by the high degree of informality and low level of organisation of the area and its features. A garden shed or garage spilled debris, usually of the husband's activities, into the yard, children's toys littered it, and the vegetable patch was designed for efficient cultivation rather than for its appearance. On a good day the backyard could be neat and tidy but never pretty or inviting. The general impression it created was rural rather than urban, particularly so in those many backyards that included a chicken pen or a rabbit hutch tucked away in a back corner.

The usage of this backyard varied, depending upon one's position in the family. The parents would not normally entertain their friends there, but children were usually *instructed* to do so there rather than in the house. Children would use it for play; however, despite its relative indestructibility, it would still be a site of more or less constant parental supervision and so usually used as a springboard into the more exciting areas of the street or the local vacant bit of land or bush. The parents tended to use the backyard as a place of domestic work: hanging out the washing, home repairs, gardening and so on. Probably the member of the family who made most use of the backyard as an 'outdoor living area' was the family dog or cat, and this fact gives some indication of the degree of change in the transformation that has occurred to bring the backyard into the structure exemplified in Artisan's 'Rembrandt'.

The distinctiveness of the backyard is thrown into sharper relief when we compare it with the kind of front garden that normally accompanied it—the front garden dominant in the 1950s in Australian suburbia. The front garden was, as Geoffrey Bolton puts it in *Spoils and Spoilers*, the 'conventional but deeply important means of self-expression for most Australian suburban dwellers':

> This was the private environment in which many dedicated their weekends to the care and maintenance of lawns and flower beds which still followed English canons of taste. Around neatly manicured patches of grass Iceland poppies, delphiniums, and, above all, roses were cherished and lavishly watered. [p. 130]

As Bolton says, native plants were held in 'scant respect'. The gardens were controlled, bordered, European, and definitively 'culture' rather than 'nature'. There were paths to keep one off the lawn, gates to inhibit entry, and picket fences or low walls to separate the garden from the footpath on the street. The relatively unadorned grass verge between footpath and street was called the 'nature strip' in some states, making the nature–culture division between the garden and the verge absolutely explicit.

Although such features asserted the privacy of the property, the display the garden provided was for the consumption of those in the street, for public rather than for private use. Exactly as in the contemporary home, the front garden was rarely used by the family, who occupied it primarily to maintain it—a time-consuming task given the exotic nature of the plants found within it. The only sense of this display area being anything other than hermetically sealed off from human use was derived from the tendency of the driveway at its side to carry some of the meanings of the backyard, as it leaked on to the drive through the garage, the car or the back entrance to the house.

The recurrence of some of the oppositions of nature with culture, and public with private, is clear, and it illustrates how furtively Australianness is invoked at this point in our cultural history. Where the front garden gestured towards Europe, the backyard was Australian. Where the front garden was public in its display, renouncing private uses, the backyard was private and useful, seeming to deny the whole idea of public display. Where the front garden was urban or suburban, the backyard was closer to the rural. Where the front garden was carefully cultured, the backyard was naturally neglected. Where the front garden was determined by canons of middle-class decency and taste, the backyard seemed to effortlessly disregard them in the name of practicality. And front and back signified an opposition between adults and children, an opposition that is signified in different ways in the contemporary house, though now internalised and concealed within the walls of the home itself.

The fundamental oppositions seem familiar, but there are some significant shifts. The backyard was not aspiring to incorporate nature as part of a public social display. Instead it accepted the reality of an exploitative attitude to the natural, defoliating and domesticating it to form the vegie patch, the chook run and the big kids' play pen. The front was more the site of the 'natural', but nature as defined in other national (English) and class terms. The backyard, with its lack of systematic control and neglect of imposed standards of taste, came closer to an indigenous Australian discourse, a particular discourse of Australianness which constructed the family and the nation in its own specific ways.

We can see the coexistence of both kinds of garden on the one suburban plot as a sign of the shallowness of the commitment to English values embodied in the front garden, as well as the lack of confidence in the values less consciously articulated in the backyard. The same sort of contradiction and ambivalence can be seen in the policies of the Menzies government in the 1950s and 1960s, when the Anglophile Menzies (Knight of the Order of the Thistle and later Warden of the Cinque Ports) presided over a profound shift economically and politically away from British hegemony. Significantly, in the previous decade the Labour Prime Minister Curtin had used the metaphor of the backyard to justify withdrawing Australian troops from the European theatre.

One of the important changes that have occurred within the suburban garden is this reduction of the signifiers of Englishness and the increasing sense of confidence in the developing 'canons of taste' of indigenous Australia. One of the most important factors in such a perception is the change in the sort of plants being used in gardens—the dramatic reversal of attitudes to Australian plants—and the images of the bush that live metaphorically in our sleepers, woodchips, groundcovers and rustic paving. Underlying it all is the idea that Europe (or England) is culture, and Australia is nature. The recent cultural shift towards Australianness is justified by reading it as a shift towards the natural.

The introduction of native plants was partly enclosed within other cultural movements which produced paving, trees planted for shade, woodchips, and so on. These are the weapons of low-maintenance gardening, assisting the recovery of the garden for leisure rather than work. This phenomenon is by no means confined to Australia. American, particularly West Coast, gardens have responded to this, too, and in fact a great deal of our history of suburban living can be seen to derive from or be paralleled by movements in California. More generally, however, the separation of leisure from work is a feature of the contemporary construction of our world and is visible in the changing signifiers of 'lifestyle' available in television advertising where work has become all but invisible. The inscription of the concept of leisure into the home has not just affected changes in gardens but also generated new structures such as games rooms, family rooms and the pool area.

These changes, however, can't be read as a simple triumph of Australian nationalism or a new easy acceptance of nature. The modern 'native' garden is more natural and Australian than the 1950s English-style front garden, but the loss of the backyard is the loss of a distinctively Australian set of meanings, which affirmed working-class and rural, if not natural, ways of living. Even if some elements of the backyard, such as the vegetable plot, are now staging a comeback, its contemporary version is part of a different structure of meanings, connected not to work but to a middle-class interest in vegetarianism, whole foods and 'health' as a lifestyle. The institution of the chook pen, too, has been the victim of civilisation's takeover of the backyard. The chook pen is now in the category of the 'dirty'—the side of nature that is deemed impossible to acculturate and thus a subject of control. The chook pen is untidy, brings rats, creates noise (the rooster's crow is natural from one point of view, but noise pollution from another) and is further seen to be residual evidence of lower-class position and aspirations and is thus eschewed by upwardly mobile families.

This system of negotiations has some effect on what the suburban garden says about those who live in it, specifically on how it constructs the family. The family as a single cohesive unit has been written into the outdoor living area, and while the children still have their places within it—more specific and contained spaces than before—the inscription of the parents and their friends is a major result of the transformation. In the new version the relational split between parents and children is smoothed over, expressing the current official ideology of parent–child relations (we no longer profess to believe that children are to be seen and not heard). In the barbecue, the outdoor eating area, and even in games rooms and pools, we have an assertion of the cohesion and unity of the family unit rather than a demarcation of differences between young and old, parents and children—all this at a time when the prophets of doom are lamenting the breakdown of the family unit, pointing to figures on divorce, drug addiction, schoolgirl pregnancies and other signs of fracture of the nuclear family. The divergence between hard figures and semiotic forms, however, is not an irreconcilable contradiction. It is precisely on occasions when a fundamental institution is most under threat that it will most insistently project images of harmony and control, in order to legitimate itself and reconstitute its former basis.

Another marker of the change between the 1950s and the 1980s can be seen in the family pet, an important occupant of the backyard/outdoor living area. Although the ubiquity of the family pet is unchanged, the nature of these pets is not. Those of us over 40 grew up in the heyday of the fox terrier and the kelpie cross. Today's children have labradors, setters, retrievers, poodles, silkies, and so on. Pedigrees have made nonsense of the saying 'it's a dog's life'. As part of the backyard, pets were most consistently linked with the children of the family. Fox terriers were popular because they were 'good with kids', as were, to a lesser degree, labradors and cocker spaniels. Pedigreed dogs of other breeds, signifiers of class and individuality if not of outright elitism, were rare in Australian suburbia 30 years ago. Now it is the terrier who is rare, the cocker spaniel has gone the way of high-maintenance gardens (its floppy ears used to pick up grass seeds and ticks, with real facility), and their places have been taken by other dogs. These new breeds, too, are often selected as children's pets although they often require training for this role rather than fit naturally into it. So now the family pet can be a Doberman pinscher, a German shepherd, or more exotic breeds such as the Rhodesian ridgeback, the red setter or the Afghan. The dogs listed have very different connotations to the terrier, or the labrador, even: the pet has become a prized possession, its degree of importance deriving from its rarity and thus its cost. Like a key object in the living room, it is a signifier of class, of status, of the capacity for conspicuous consumption, and of complicated expressions of individual taste within these social parameters.

Highly bred dogs are, like highly bred people, indexes of the superiority of culture over nature. Accordingly, it is possible to see this trend in pets as an expression of the same general pattern that transformed the backyard into the outdoor living area. The terrier and the kelpie are essentially rural and, in the kelpie's case, working dogs which are kept for a purpose that was practical and pastoral but not otherwise directly expressive of the family.

The new breed of pet signifies European or colonial culture, in its evocation of the pets of the aristocratic and the rich in Europe. This is even more evident in the stray tabby cat's capitulation to the exotic breeds such as the Siamese or the Burmese. The highly bred cat, even more than the dog, connotes European class and luxury. Because of their value, such cats are not the children's possessions (except perhaps as kittens) but tend to be associated with women as domestic companions and indexes of surplus wealth—as a current series of commercials for Whiskas suggests in its identification of cats exclusively with their female owners, seeing them as surrogate, simplified children and their feeding as part of the motherly role of the suburban middle-class housewife.

Changes like these provide us with complex maps of meaning in the developing process of definition of such a thing as the 'Australian' suburban home. On the one hand, the rejection of European values seems healthy and confident, proposing new and more appropriate ways of explaining and constructing Australian life than those handed on to us by a parent culture. On the other hand, the acceleration in the rate of the inscription of status and of generally materialist middle-class values into what are also 'Australian' structures hints at the likely character of the indigenous challenges we may face in the future. In general, however, the kinds of changes we can see indicate an effective process of dealing with the environmental determinants of our lives in Australia and a growing readiness to admit these into our ways of living that is productive, realistic and often imaginative. If 'imaginative' or 'creative' are not words normally associated with a description of suburban living in Australia, that is due to the poverty of cultural analysis of the society to date and its inability to even hint at the reasons why most Australians make sense of their lives within that most maligned of environments, suburbia.

3   The Beach

The Meanings of the Beach

> How right Neville Shute was to set the end of the world on the beach. Speaking as a human shipwreck, beached on the soul-destroying sands, I regard the gritty fringe of the continent as purgatorial and hellish. Given that life spent billions of years struggling out of the oceans, aspiring to the comparative civilisation of dry land, it seems both eccentric and blasphemous for the majority of Australians to put evolution into reverse. Our lemming-like rush from hinterland to high tide, from prime real estate to primal ooze suggests we've all got sunstroke.
>
> —Phillip Adams

The epigraph from Phillip Adams derives its force from its direct opposition to what has become a national institution, the beach. For the modern Australian, according to its 'quality' weekly voice, the *National Times*, 'Australia *means* [emphasis added] the beach'. In this chapter we shall look at the specific meanings of the beach in Australian culture.

Here we can extend the categories used in the previous chapter's discussion of gardens and outdoor living in the suburban home. Much more than the acculturated version of the natural in the out-door living area, the beach is uncompromisingly seen within the general framework of the natural, the free, the outdoors, the infor-mal, the physical, and so on. Phillip Adams' position (made clear in his opposing the beach to civilisation) is to deny the value of this way of seeing the beach by drawing on an alternative ideology of rationalism: supporting culture over nature, the civilised over the primitive, the intellectual over the physical. Adams here is not proposing the dominant ideology; he extravagantly rejects a point of view that prefers the healthy to the unhealthy, the natural to the unnatural, the robust to the effete, and finally the Australian to the unAustralian.

The beach's centrality to the culture is won by its appropriation of those attitudes most closely related to an Australian mythology while placing itself in opposition to those that are excluded. This may be fairly obvious. However, the beach—our great natural playground—is also usually, and paradoxically, a city beach and the most well-known and often-cited examples are those that are anything but natural in context: Bondi, Surfers, Manly, and so on. In order to more fully understand the cultural function of the beach we need to examine the ways in which, while drawing so heavily on the natural, it manages to fit so seamlessly into its urban context (culture) without losing its potential for its primary meaning (nature).

If small farmers on their selections in the backblocks, and the image of the pioneer on the land provide the central myths for traditional Australia, modern Australia has its own myths. One involves suburbia—less fashionable since the 1950s and Barry Humphries/Edna Everage—and the other the beach. The beach's elevation to significance has a number of historical determinants, two of them being the growth of public mixed bathing and the growth of mass transportation. More importantly, however, the beach's increasing centrality to Australian myths coincides—paradoxically, it may seem—with an increasing urbanisation. As the free, natural, and tough bush existence became more obviously an anachronistic version of national identity, the figure of the bronzed lifesaver filled the gap. If Australia meant, among other things, closeness with a harsh but still bountiful nature, such meanings could not be found in the city—unless it was on the surf beaches. So, as the bushman became less relevant to modern Australia, the ideology which once mythologised him, valuing his harmony with the natural environment and his tough physicality, now supports the beach. Consequently the central image of the Australian beach is *not* that of the tropical hideaway. That does exist, but is reserved for holidays, preferably outside Australia. The beach that contributes to everyday existence must be metropolitan, therefore urban. It is Bondi Beach, with its rows of hotels and fast food outlets; Manly, with its aquarium and dodgem cars; or the most recent additions, cities that are planned solely in order to be close to the beach thus clearly highlighting the relation between beach and city: Surfers Paradise, or the Western Australian version where the relationship is openly admitted in the name of Yanchep Sun City.

The meaning of the Australian beach, then, can be located in at least two apparently contradictory paradigms; one places it within the category of the environment of the city, making it intrinsic to it and therefore 'culture'; the other sees it in the category of the 'natural', the alternative (or even in opposition) to the comfortable security of the suburb. Manly or Cottesloe are the beach made city-like, suburbanised: the wild surf beaches, often unnamed, untamed, are the alternatives offered by nature. The beaches that most clearly stand for the dominant myth of the Australian beach—Bondi, Surfers Paradise—accept both meanings simultaneously, effectively setting up a new paradigm which is made up of natural 'beachness' and 'Australian metropolitan beachness'. This new paradigm is the characteristically Australian beach which is urban *and* natural, civilised *and* primitive, spiritual *and* physical, culture *and* nature. The meaning of any one beach is a particular example of this paradigm, as either culture or nature is subordinated in favour of its opposite.

The codes of regulated urban existence and those of the natural and informal differ most where nature is at its most uncompromising: on the surf beaches. There is consequently a hierarchy, at the head of which is the surf. Like the outback, the surf challenges the user and does so more vigorously than do the harbour beaches of Sydney or the bay beaches of Adelaide, Brisbane and Melbourne; the surf is ultimately definitive of the Australian beach. To go to 'the beach' in Adelaide, Brisbane or Melbourne is not to go to Glenelg, Redcliffe or Brighton. In all these cities, one has to travel some distance to the coast, and in Brisbane's case to another city/ beach, Surfers Paradise. For those suburban, safe beaches still within the city limits, it is a necessary part of their appeal that they still contain echoes of the thrill and freedom of the surf. As we shall see the risk may be absent, but the link, however minimal, remains.

The surf beach develops a 'fundamentalist' youth subculture of its own with its own codes and practices that oppose the conventions of more normal society; we will examine this further in the following section. In the wider culture's use of the beach, the rituals are highly conventionalised, impregnated with clues to status and community role distinctions. This determines the characters given to the individual beaches themselves, encouraging fine discrimination. If the paradigm we describe exists, there are a multitude of selections and combinations drawn from it. Not all beaches are the same, not all spots on the same beach are the same. Walking from Bondi to North Bondi, or over to Tamarama, for instance, takes one through the spectrum of occasional, day-tripper beachgoers to the hard-core aficionados whose tans signify their membership of an elite. Such a geographical hierarchy at Cronulla is described by Gabrielle Carey and Kathy Lette in *Puberty Blues*:

> There were three main sections of Cronulla Beach—South Cronulla, North Cronulla, and Greenhills.
> That's where the top surfies hung out—the prettiest girls from school and the best surfies on the beach. The bad surfboard riders on their 'L' plates, the Italian family groups and the 'uncool' kids from Bankstown (Bankies), swarmed to South Cronulla—Dickheadland. That's where it all began. We were dickheads. [p. 1]

Greenhills is the furthest away, the place where the fewest concessions are made to city comforts, where the beach is the main attraction. Similarly in Tamarama, there are no permanent kiosks, no parking, no amusement parlours, and the surf is particularly rough.

Because the beach signifies both its intrinsic oneness with the city and also its otherness, the ways in which any particular accommodation with the urban context is mediated provides us with access to particular meanings, a particular relation to its users, and any one beach's particular relation to the mythic Australian beach. For instance, Sydney's harbour beaches (where there is no surf) tend to have no barriers around them in the form of railings or fences, so apparently, open access is invited. However, they do tend to be hidden away: Chinaman's Beach is approached by way of a grassy picnic ground off the main road, and the beach itself is hidden by dunes covered with grass. Camp Cove is approached by way of a small gateway, and like Chinaman's its facilities for car parking are drastically limited. Such beaches are known to be exclusive, and their placement produces a relatively regulated access. At such beaches the natural is subordinated to the city and the community, as the sand and sea are seen as material extensions of an urban community of property owners who 'have' the location of the entrance. The main activity on these beaches revolves around boats and dogs as much as swimming or tanning. There are carloads

Beach luxury

By PAUL PATERSON

Units are ideal for nature lovers

AN ATTRACTIVE combination of location and design are features of a new luxury residential development in Rockingham.

The two town houses and two villas in Fletcher Street are 50 metres from Palm Beach and offer views of Garden Island and Mangles Bay.

The double-storey town houses are priced at $82,500 and the villas at $80,000.

Boating facilities and a park are adjacent to the development, which will attract nature lovers.

All the units overlook a tidal lagoon which is a breeding area for a variety of sea birds.

Traffic past the development is restricted because Fletcher Street is not a through road.

Each unit has private front and rear courtyards, patio, garage, reticulated gardens and built-in robes.

Slate-tiled

The three-bedroom villas offer an attractive blend of luxury and common sense.

Architects Oldfield and Knott decided that the villas should have slate-tiled entrances instead of carpets to make cleaning easier after a visit to the beach.

The villas feature exposed beams in the living and dining room areas, tumble clothes dryers, dishwashers and drive-through garages.

The double-storey town houses are bigger than the villas and have better views.

Upstairs there are three bedrooms, a bathroom and a balcony off the master bedroom. The kitchen, laundry, dining and living area are downstairs.

Extras include a laundry chute, reticulated gardens, dryer and dishwasher.

The beach and the city meet in this commercial for 'town-houses' for nature-lovers. The confusion of the trappings of urban living (high-technology appliances, high-density housing) and 'natural' features (close to boating, sea birds, etc.) make the advertisement an excellent example of the ways in which the beach is made part of the *urbs*.

of expensive outdoor furniture brought on to the beach, domesticating it and transforming it into a backyard or balcony. The beach on Camp Cove and similar places transforms nature into high-density urban accommodation—itself signified by the complex mixture of the natural and the cultural which recalls the line from an Australian Crawl song 'the garden's full of furniture, and the house is full of plants'. Anti-egalitarian in the formality of access, highly 'civilised' (even explicitly European) in the practices on the beach, their forms and functions deny their Australian 'beachness' and thus distance themselves from the myth by which Australians like to imagine they understand the beach. The fact that so many beaches differ from the myth shows, perhaps, how the myth is rooted in an ideal (that is, one not necessarily made material on any one beach) image of Australia—classless, matey, basic, natural—rather than a more realistic apprehension of our urban, artificially structured society.

Sydney's most populous surf beaches, unlike the more classy harbour ones, tend to be spread brashly in front of the public, implying unlimited and casual access—an egalitarianism of form and function. The esplanade is often without guard rails, offering the chance of jumping on to the sand at any point. At some beaches, such as Coogee, the esplanade's height above the sand does discriminate in favour of the fit and the robust. Unlike Chinaman's the surf beaches usually make little attempt to mediate between sand and pavement; the transition from city to nature is abrupt, unmediated and therefore emphasised. The surf beach is offered as a bald challenge to the urban environment of which it is a part, and is spread out uninterrupted with the road dutifully following the contours of the sand. Rarely is the vista of the beach interrupted by houses, hotels, funfairs or the like.

In contrast, the bay beaches of Melbourne and Adelaide are heavily built out with shops and houses, the beach owning up to its meagre existence (no surf, or, in Melbourne's case, inferior sand) by only occasional formal entrance points. Unlike the exclusivity of Chinaman's, this kind of formal entrance is apologetic; it assumes one enters only if one cannot avoid it. (Public pools are consequently more popular in Melbourne than Sydney.) By default, since they lack all the virtues and attributes of the mythic, ideal Australian beach, such beaches are less natural, less informal, and therefore prefer the urban, civilised side of the dialectic. Curiously, and for different reasons, the beaches at Surfers Paradise are built out, too, the buildings shading the beach in the afternoon and indicating that the attractions of the urbs are insistently proposing themselves as equally important to those of the beach. Further down the Gold Coast, however, this pattern changes, and the beaches where urban development is less dense still foreground their naturalness, their sense of being the main attraction.

So the ways in which the particular beach is placed in relation to its context determine the kind of relationship it has to the archetypal Australian beach, the kind of meanings it generates, and therefore the kinds of uses to which it will be put. It is these meanings that semiotics makes available to us.

Semiotically, the beach can be read as a text. Like all texts, the beach has an author; not, admittedly, a named individual, but an historically determined set of community practices that have produced material objects or signs. These include the beach-side buildings, the changing rooms, the lawns, the esplanades, the vendors' kiosks, the regulatory notices, the steps and benches, the flags and litter-bins—all these items whose foregrounded functional dimensions should not blind us to their signifying one. Like all texts, beaches have readers. In their choice of their beach, people use beaches to seek out certain kinds of meanings for themselves, meanings that help them come to terms with their usual off-beach lifestyle. As with other texts, these meanings are determined partly by the structure of the text itself and partly by the social and individual characteristics of the reader—different people use the beach differently (they find different meanings in it), but there is a core of meanings that all users, from respectable suburban families to drop-out surfers, share to a greater or lesser extent.

The beach is neither land nor sea, but has some characteristics of both. It therefore carries the meanings of both and is thus almost 'overloaded' with potential meanings. It is, as structural anthropologists call it, an 'anomalous' category, in the middle of the basic oppositions of the culture from which we construct our meanings—such as 'them' and 'us', 'good' and 'bad', the land and the sea. Structural anthropologists have shown how anomalous creatures gain special significance, of magic or the supernatural in some cases: the centaur is anomalous between man and beast, an angel (or Christ) between man and god, the fox between the domestic and the wild.

Let us start by exploring the beach's role as an anomalous category between land and sea. The physical layout of the beach may seem without significance—didn't nature design this?; analysis suggests this may not be so. The beach provides a physical bridge between the city (culture) and the sea (nature). In the illustration below, we show diagrammatically how the beach serves this mediating function. It is a representation of the structure of a typical beach.

The move from culture, the city, on the right to nature, the sea, on the left is effected through a number of zones. First there is the road, the public site of transition, and the boundary beyond which the car, that crucial cultural motif, cannot pass. Next comes grass, or more typically and significantly, lawn. Lawns invoke the natu-

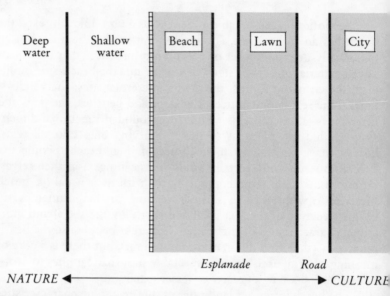

The zones of the beach

ral, not nature: so it is appropriate that on them we find 'furniture': benches, which are either painted green to look 'natural' or left as 'natural' wood. The lawn is the most cultured bit of the beach and may be most typically used by the old, or families with young children, who need the security of culture, or perhaps some shade to protect them from the sun. We may also find those we could uncharitably type the incorrigibly suburban who import their chairs, tables, rugs, trannies and sometimes even television to make the outdoors as much like indoors as possible. Although we may find the occasional group of sunbakers here, for most of its users this zone provides an easy transition towards nature. At the edge of the lawn we meet the esplanade, a concrete flat-topped wall that marks the boundary beyond which the sea is not allowed to come: like all boundaries it is a popular place to walk, a moment of balance in a sacred no-man's-land outside profane normality.

The use of the esplanade underlines an important proviso to the 'zonal' structure of the beach. The zones are vague, the boundaries ill-marked, if not unmarked, and consequently the categories and their meanings leak one into the other. Very close to the esplanade is one narrow zone, and this provides one set of meanings that serves different functions for at least two very different sorts of

The browning of Australia

ROSE SHAPIRO, an English journalist, looks at the peculiar Australian passion for the perfect tan, and, below, GINA SCHIEN gives a guide to the cheapest of the best sunscreens.

Tanning naturally. The illustration and heading of a full-page article in the *National Times*, 19 December, 1982.

people. What they have in common is a negative: they do not see swimming as the main purpose of their visit to the beach. One group is the dressed mothers and fathers with the undressed children; this group will also be found on the lawn, and for them the meaning of the beach is centred on the home and family (i.e. culture) rather than in nature. The other group is that of the sun-bakers, and their meaning, though articulated differently, is surprisingly similar to the suburban family's.

A tan, too, is an anomalous category falling between *skin* (human, culture) and *fur* (animal, nature). A tanned body is a sign to be read by others, particularly others in the city. It signifies that the wearer, a city dweller, has been into nature and is bringing back both the physical health of the animal, but also the mental health that contact with nature brings into the artificiality of city life. The first signifying function of the tan is to bring the natural into culture. The natural is not 'nature', but the culture's construction of it, and thus the tan is achieved via a number of cultural commodities, not least of which are barriers, or screens that protect the body from the dangers of the sun, raw nature, in the same way as the esplanade protects the land from the dangers of the sea. This natural meaning of the tan has also, as do all signs in our culture, a class dimension.

The *National Times* (December 19–25, 1982) devoted a whole page to an article about suntanning and sunscreening. The illustration is significant. The topless sunbaker is middle class—the hat and the connotations of the style of drawing are adequate class markers. Her (dark) tan needs to be differentiated from the black servant whose colour, by contrast, signals the whiteness (racial) of the sunbaker, and whose class is also part of the signification of the tan. The accompanying article points out that solarium tans cost up to $65 to acquire, natural tans of the required quality take up to ten hours' sunbaking a day, sunscreens cost on average $4. Sunbeds are used by 'busy working ladies with no time to go to the beach', obviously to signal their desired, if false, membership of the true bourgeoisie, which is a leisured bourgeoisie.

The tan, with its connotations of leisure, money, sophistication, meanings for others, must be significantly distinguished from the colour achieved by the outdoor manual worker; and of course it is, by its smoothness and texture and by its evenness over all (or nearly all) parts of the body. As the *National Times* puts it, 'it turns out to be all too easy to obtain the uneven coloration deprecatingly termed a 'farmers's tan'. It takes time and commitment to get the all-over allure of a deep and enduring brownness'. The naturalness of tan serves to naturalise class: leisure, money and an attitude of mind are creators of meaning that provide access to the natural.

To move from the area occupied by the serious tanners, on to the central zone of the beach, which is the strip nearest the sea, is to find some of the same categories of users we noted elsewhere: families, suntanners, and so on. Their relation to the sea is less ambiguous because it is less mediated. They tend to be more active, physical—natural. It is here we find the swimmers, the games players, the joggers, clustered at the edge of the next boundary, the sea. The degree of congregation—around popular spots or between the flags—points to the need for further mediation before entering the sea. It is at this position that the opposition between land and sea, nature and culture, is most openly confronted, admitted and (usually) celebrated.

Variations and particularisations of these general patterns may be observed in the full range of Australian beaches. Before leaving this typical urban beach, however, we should note the other signifying structures it contains: the signs prohibiting dogs or surfboards; the flags which mark those areas of the beach under cultural supervision; the civic facilities such as bins and benches; the

Topless or even nude bathing is becoming the norm on many Australian beaches. Shedding clothes may be shedding culture, but culture rarely lets its control slip completely. Here it struggles against nudity's naturalness by giving it meanings of voyeurism and thus ensuring its place in a male-dominated culture. The beach legitimates the display of the body and the pleasure of the voyeur.

But it also defies these meanings. Nude bathing is defiantly non-sexist; bodies are understood not as attractive for others, but as sources of pleasure for their owners. The topless sunbaker ignores or even challenges the male gaze (and wins when the man averts his eyes or pretends not to look). Shedding clothes and shedding culture can deny the male role of looking and the female of being looked at.

A sign of changing attitudes is the gradual disappearance of the beauty contest (the epitome of licensed voyeurism) from our beaches in the face of the new meanings of gender and gender relations that the normalisation of nudity is bringing. Major beauty contests are now held in lavish function centres before TV cameras. But a one-piece bathing suit is still the defining marker of the Beauty Queen, a quotation from a more cultured form of sexism from a more congenial past.

pavilion, offering further urban amenities. Such items underline how far away the beach we have been using as our text, Cottesloe in Perth, is from the ideal constructions of the beach that Craig McGregor gives in the *National Times* (9 January 1983): 'a beach with no houses, no tents, no sandmining, no road and no way in except in bare feet, or maybe in thongs, bikini and sunvisor . . . you can swim naked there. Only albino sandcrabs and, occasionally, a gaggle of surfboard riders to keep you company'. This list is diametrically opposed to that of the city beach, but the dream of this ideal beach is nonetheless the source of the urban beach's appeal. The urban beach, particularly the safer, suburban beach, may have only a symbolic connection with the ideal, isolated beach of nature, but it is a crucial symbolic connection.

Most of us do not want to move all that far away from culture. Jo Kennedy, the actress/ singer who was cast away with Mike Willesee and two others on a tropical island for a TV documentary on survival, expressed a common perception. Standing on a huge deserted 'ideal' beach she complained: 'I miss the beach—the proper beach, with suntan oil and towels.' Just as the house is the displacement of the small farm in the bush, the urban and suburban beach defines its central mythic role in modern Australia as a result of complex negotiations between the ideal beach of nature and the material culture of the city.

Lifesavers, Surfers and Anomalous Categories

The opposing meanings of the beach, one set veering towards nature, the other towards culture, became personified in the rivalry between surfer and lifesaver. Historically the lifesaver has dominated our mythology of the beach, for the surfer only reached significance in the 1950s. Surfing as a pastime, however, grew in popularity between the wars. At that time the Australian refinement of 'bathing' in the sea was more the act of 'body surfing' than the use of the surfboard. This kind of surfing became institutionalised through the establishment of surf lifesaving clubs, which, although dating back to the period just before the Great War, came into their own in the 1930s. The lifesaver quickly became the paragon of national manhood, and the clubs attracted members effortlessly for the next twenty years. The legendary status they achieved, a status enhanced by such exploits as the mass rescue of 200 swimmers off Bondi in February 1938, spawned a large body of social practices and structures which then became part of the rituals of the Australian beach. Surf carnivals, rescue drills, the shark bell or whistle, the system of surfing 'between the flags', and the privileged, custodial position accorded to the men wearing coloured caps are features of the Australian day at the beach.

These days, however, the lifesaver is not quite the central figure he once was on our beaches. If he is still an heroic figure rowing out to scare sharks from the urban beaches, his heroism is counterpointed and qualified by the few surfers suicidally straddling their boards further out to sea, affecting a nonchalant disinterest in the proceedings. The surfer is the bane of the lifesaver's life, ignoring the flags and signs on the beach, threatening swimmers with injury from loose boards, requiring regulations to bring him under community control, and even introducing unwelcome influences into the local surfclub dance. The surfers might be the contemporary version of the lifesavers in their ubiquity on our beaches, but in all other respects they are their antithesis, both in the use they make of the beach and in the myths upon which that use is predicated.

Essentially, and to continue the dialectic we have highlighted, the lifesaver brings culture on to the beach. Not only is he metonymic of the city—particularly Sydney—and thus culture, but the practices that develop around the lifesaving clubs are those of the most disciplined of institutional structures—the military. Lifesavers have drills, march-pasts, and patrol squads, while exercising a conservative pastoral interest in their members' moral health. They are agents of social control. Further, they see themselves as servants of the community, sacrificing their weekends for others—a tradition of sacrifice dear to a nation which twice voted *no* to conscription in the Great War. The easily constructed nobility of the calling is significant in the change of name from the American and British life*guard* to life*saver*. The change emphasises positive action, heroism, connotations of self-sacrifice, with its denial of the motives of self-indulgence and romantic self-interest that so clearly typifies the surfers' role: while lifesavers give up their time to 'patrol' the beach, surfers are seen to be indulging themselves on the beach all day whilst living on the dole. If the lifesavers are the heroes of this myth, then the surfers are its anti-heroes.

What lifesavers have done is to civilise Australia's beaches, to transform them into safe urban areas by standing between the beachgoer and the dangers of nature. They did this with the flags, the ambulance service, by manning the icecream kiosk, by providing the beachgoers with continual pop music booming out over the club's public address system, and—at the last—by the rescue. The entire environment was metaphorically transformed into a swimming pool by the flag, the cap, the line and the whistle. Australia responded by according the lifesaver the kind of heroic status accorded the digger. In 1938, for the sesquicentenary celebrations in Sydney, lifesavers joined in the 'March to Nationhood' pageant, filling the role—as Richard White points out in *Inventing Australia*—of the shearers in 1901 and the diggers after Gallipoli. Similarly, when Queen Elizabeth made her first royal tour of Australia in 1954, she attended a surf carnival as part of her initiation into the central aspects of Australian culture. That might seem unremarkable, unless we tried to imagine her being treated to a board-riding contest as part of the royal tour today. If the myth of the beach does involve the superimposition of culture on nature, then the lifesaver occupies an important role in the processes by which this has been achieved.

The surfer is altogether different, historically and semiotically. Instead of emerging from the flux of nationalism and the search for the 'Australian type' that dominated the turn of the century and which takes much of the blame for the rush to enlist for the First World War, the surfer emerged from the flurry of largely American activity that invented the teenager, rock'n'roll and the juvenile delinquent in the late 1950s. By the early 1960s the Australian surfer was established as a 'problem', an oppositional cult usually paired with the even less desirable bodgie. The bodgie disappeared as fashions changed, but the surfer has not, outliving the music culture which grew up around the surf, and the essentially youth-oriented myth that surrounded its heroes. The early surf heroes, the Midge Farrellys and the Nat Youngs, went on to become successful businessmen, albeit in the romantic cottage-industry manner of the surfers' commodity markets. Surfers adopted dress and behaviour that challenged the conventions of good manners and the politics of the occasion—lifestyles that by their frank hedonism exposed the hypocrisy of the materialist parent culture; and most importantly their chosen mode of existence displaced work from its central place as the primary social role of the Australian citizen. The surfer in Australia has articulated and developed the most coherent and continuous discourse of opposition to the dominant, and is unique amongst the subcultures of youth.

In Australian patterns of representation of the two groups, if the lifesaver is culture, the surfer is nature; if the lifesaver is responsible, law-abiding and community spirited, the surfer is irresponsible, feckless and 'a bludger'; if the lifesaver is civilised, the surfer is primitive; the lifesaver is the land, the surfer the sea. And despite the attempts of the dominant culture to appropriate the imagery of surfing as in Coke advertisements and the brand name of a washing powder, thus incidentally seeking to undermine the subversive significance of the surfer, the subculture still maintains its romantic position outside the dominant ideology.

The surfer is not unique to Australia—Southern California and parts of South Africa have similar cultural practices and figures—but he occupies an area within our youth culture in which, under the umbrella of the myth of youth culture which is largely international, an indigenous discourse has been most fully developed. We find the details of this discourse, these particularisations of the myth of the youth, available to us semiotically as we examine the practices that articulate the myth of the surfer in Australia.

Youth, like the beach, is an anomalous category, the one between child and adult. The surfers, too, are anomalous, lying between the solid citizen and the criminal. Their whole subculture is riddled with this kind of status; they spend their time on the anomalous beach, acquiring an anomalous tan, mispending their anomalous youth, riding their anomalous surfboards, and driving their anomalous vehicles. It is appropriate that this accumulation of meaning of beach, youth, surfboard, and panel van should have elements of the sacred for its initiates and of the taboo for the rest. We will turn our attention first to the panel van, a uniquely Australian vehicle and therefore an active indicator to the meanings of its users.

The panel van is ambiguous in that it has got the form of a truck for work, but it is used more like a car for leisure and for other social/sexual purposes. It is mass produced, and yet individualised as if to deny its mass production. But the individualisation is, in fact, highly conventional. The differences between different panel vans are differences of the signifier only. All vans share the same signified, that of male youth defining his meaning as neither child nor adult. The owners have to have reached a certain age to own one, to be able to afford one and to be allowed to drive one legally. They are defining themselves as not children. Yet they are also not adult. This customising is expensive and conspicuously wasteful, which defines them as not the young adult who is typically saving up money to be married or to put down the deposit on a house, or a mortgage. The conspicuous consumption cuts off the panel van, both from the younger and from the older.

Further, even though individualised panel vans are works of

art, they are significantly differentiated from the traditional role of art in the capitalist society, which, as the French sociologist Pierre Bourdieu has shown, serves social status and class differentiation, as well as economic capital. Panel van art certainly has status and class functions, though they serve a deviant, not the dominant group, but where panel van art most importantly differs from fine art is in its investment role. Panel vans are essentially disposable art. They are not going to last very much longer. By their very nature, they can't. So it is almost as though this is a perfect youth art because as youth isn't going to last, so is the art form not going to last. And this differentiates it, sets up a significant difference between this and the function of fine art in the straight older culture.

The panel van is also anomalous between indoors and outdoors. It is furnished like a house with carpets, decorations, hi-fi systems, mattresses, cushions, and yet it is outdoors as well. Its furnishings are designed for sexual adventures, which are again part of the deviance of youth, between the non-sexual child and the married, sexually bonded adult. There is a strong association between panel vans and drive-ins, itself an ambiguous location. When a panel van is in a drive-in, the owners have to signify their difference from the straight family viewer by reversing the vehicle, so that the panel vans are all parked oppositionally to the family cars. Now we know there is a function for this, in that it enables sex and cinema to be enjoyed at the same time. But the functional dimension is never the only one in social behaviour—there is always a signifying one: in this case, of establishing difference from the family composed of adults and children. So the cultural connections, the signifying similarities, between panel vans and beach and youth, are not coincidental. They are all part of the way that a culture, its various manifestations and informal institutions, fit together into the sort of ideological system that Louis Althusser called 'overdetermination', the word having the sense of 'oversee' rather than 'overcharge'.

On top of the panel van, as it is driven to the beach, is typically a surfboard. The surfboard is perhaps the perfect example of a category which is anomalous between nature and culture. It is carefully designed with a scientific approach to the placement of fins and the shape of the hull, yet it is also the most minimal object that enables man to float on the sea. The skill and art of the surfer resemble more the way a dolphin interacts with the sea or a bird with the air rather than man's more normal technological imposition of his will and needs upon nature, typified by the modern giant ships. As befits its anomalous status, the surfboard is both sacred and taboo. To the surfer it is an object of near worship: and there are taboos that prevent girls, or the too-young or the old from riding it. These taboos are now under attack, and girls, in particular, are beginning to be accepted as board riders.

We are not interested here in a Freudian linking of the surfboard with male sexuality, but it is worth remarking on the sexist nature of most youth subcultures, where male behaviour and female behaviour are clearly distinguished, and where males are active and dominant, and females passive and subordinate. Panel vans, motor bikes, surfboards are conventionally driven/ridden by males, and the size/skill/decoration involved is part of the male status order. Females are passengers, spectators, there to be won, possessed, flaunted by the male.

Surfer writing mingles accounts of mastering waves with ones of easy mastery of girls. Surfers have an exclusive language for each, language that signals subcultural membership and excludes outsiders, language that performs the vital function of distinguishing *us* from *them*. In this language waves are tubes, rip curls, double ender pintails; females are bushies, garudas and groupies. But the key term is 'hunting' which applies equally to waves and females. 'They were sworn to the cry of *hunt it in the day, hunt it in the dark*. And brave boys keep their promises.' Hunting is where man first denotes his mastery over nature: it is the prerequisite of cooking, which, as we showed in Chapter 2, becomes the resonant metaphor for the process of culturising nature. And consequently it is seen as a natural activity; man hunting for food, hunting for females, hunting for waves, is man behaving naturally because he is acting according to his bodily needs.

This is the main point about the meaning of surfing; this meaning is to be found in the body, in physical sensation, and in the pleasure that this produces.

The language of surfing is sensational: it works through and on the senses, the body. It centres life on nouns and adjectives, the immediate perceptions of the world that relate to the body. Main verbs with their implications of purposeful actions, weighted down by the apparatus of tense and modality, carefully relating subject and object in the culturally valued world of logic, are minimised. The short sentences, the disjointed syntax, produce a world that is a mosaic of physical sensation, of bodily freedom. The body's (or

'A righthander. So fast it makes Kirra look like a beginner's wave. A small community of surfers, nestled in the cove, looking out onto the point. Arid countryside and stunted growth. No water, less shade. Sunshine, hot air and icy water. The nearest town is 100km away along corrugated gravel tracks. A national park, but no-one at the gate to collect $600 a week to surf here. Just a small group of surfers drawn together to surf one of the world's finest rights.'

Man after man they blurred high in the lip, then dropped like falcons to the depths for the blitzing bottom carve back up to forge the left rail into torqued direction shifts, half the lip exploding through the air. The state of the art. They surfed bloody well.

For the next two hours bullshit reigned from the heavens. Five wave sets, tide coming in, and *the* Sanur-bottom walls disappearing way down the reef in bending perfection. Incredible to bugger youself on a 300 metre ride then paddle out, witness to displays of power and panache in the distance—repeated wave after wave.

Sweat oozed. Like pus from a weeping wound. A smelly heat was raping my senses, bludgeoning memories of a chilly southern autumn. Oppression. Christ. Of dirt and dogs. Of guys and girls in 'Bali' singlets popping blisters in the afternoon sun.

The language of the surf

nature's) life of sensation breaks free from the control of culture; it momentarily disrupts and fractures the seamless world of sense (as opposed to sensation) that is the hallmark and raison d'etre of culture. Breaking sentence order, producing sentences without the controlling presence of a main verb, is breaking the shackles of our primary school English teacher, herself a metonym for the conflation of linguistic and social control.

The control of the sentence is a way of achieving 'pleasure' in the rather specialised meaning that theorists like Roland Barthes give it in *The Pleasure of the Text*. He writes of pleasure as 'something both revolutionary and social . . . it cannot be taken over by any collectivity, any mentality, any ideolect.' [p. 23] This resistance of pleasure to ideological control lies at the heart of Barthes' paradoxical phrase 'the politics of pleasure'.

This notion of 'the politics of pleasure' implies that the life of sensation, of the physical senses, is a way of opposing the social control of common sense, of planning and logic. The body and the senses open up a life of freedom, of the here and now, that radically opposes that proposed by school, the family, marriage or work, with their emphasis on the future, on responsibility and conforming to the social norms. Society and its institutions exert a control that the pleasure of the senses resists.

This may well explain why young people so frequently choose pastimes that derive from the pleasure of the senses—rock'n'roll, dancing, video games, surfing—and how often adults, who value control and sense, dismiss these pleasures as mindless. When the search for sensual pleasure leads to sexual promiscuity and the use of drugs other than tobacco or alcohol, adult disapproval is expressed with far greater force. The strength of the offence caused to many adults is testimony to the oppositional meanings that the pleasures of the senses seem to carry and shows how implicitly they recognise the subversive potential of the 'politics of pleasure'.

What the culture tries to do to the surf is to deny this potential radicalism. By incorporating it into TV sports news, into the advertising of banks, or aftershave, or soft drinks, or electronic hardware, it is pulling the surfer back from the brink of becoming Nature and into the comfortable security of the Natural. The conventional, comfortable signifieds that the culture industry gives to surfing not only deradicalise it, but use its potential radicalism (i.e. its closeness to nature, now misrepresented as the natural) to support the central institutions and meaning systems of the culture. Its meaning is colonised into the service of those who should be most threatened by it.

Thus, the beach and the surf are worked on by the culture so that their overflowing meanings are controlled and legitimised. The beach, physically and conceptually closer to the city, is completely colonised. The surf, through the surfer, still shows elements of resistance to this imposition of meaning by a culturally dominant class in their own interests. The potential for subversion is still there, because physically and conceptually the surf is still nearer to nature, further from the city.

Our discussion of the surfer is still enclosed, then, within the controlling myths and discourses of the beach. We can see that while the surfing beach and the suburban beach may be at opposite ends of this opposition between land/culture, on the one hand, and sea/nature, on the other, each is essential to the meaning of the other. The absence, but potential presence, of the danger, freedom, and subversion of the surf is part of the meaning of the suburban beach—the frisson caused by its potential presence (though actual absence) is a crucial part of the attraction that it holds for the suburban family. Similarly, the breaking of suburban control and safety is crucial to the surfers: their definition of themselves as *not* 'dickheads' is a crucial part of their subcultural identity.

It is this flexibility of the beach, its wide potential for meaning, that allows different sections of society to find in it different ways of articulating, different ways of relating to, this deep biblical opposition between land and sea, or the basic anthropological one between culture and nature.

4 Out of Work

As a national stereotype the Australian is not famous for enjoying work, yet the category of work is an indispensible part of the cultural complex. In Australian society, as in all others, work is the basis of economic life, the source of wealth and value, and the dominant ideological forms are very much concerned to regulate workers and the world of work. So work weaves through the fabric of Australian culture as a presence, but also as different kinds of absence and displacement: in the kinds and uses of leisure and in attitudes to not working. This chapter looks at being 'out of' work—an oblique angle, perhaps, on the meaning of work in Australia, but it reveals the way in which work has a determinate effect even on those who do not have jobs (all too many nowadays) or those who will soon be looking for one. Unlike the preceding chapters, this one looks at the mainstream of Australian popular culture from outside, from the point of view of those queueing for admission.

At the CES

Australia as a typical Western capitalist society found the great depression of the 1930s a traumatic experience, which was branded into the national psyche as part of its mythology, with specific meanings about capitalism. Essential to those meanings is a judgment on capitalism itself, a recognition of contradictions at its core. The success of capitalism is based on the 'work ethic', a glorification of hard work as essential to the dignity of human beings, but conditions of work under capitalism lead to alienation and dehumanisation. Also, as Dennis Altman has pointed out in *Rehearsals for Change*, the increasing 'consumerisation' of the worker, a process necessary to a growing economy, turns the worker away from these

73

conditions and this ethic, in favour of the objective of a leisured hedonism. Pursuit of leisure is offered as a goal, but failure to work is seen as indigence or irresponsibility. Work acquires deeply contradictory values, so that unemployment becomes the supreme deprivation or the supreme crime. The position is complicated by the equivocal relationship of the capitalist system to the social order. Marx pointed out that capitalism thrives on a body of unemployed, who function as a 'reserve army' which serves to keep those in work docile and cheap. Unemployment under capitalism is structural, not an accident or imperfection. Yet to offer itself as a system that has the best interests of society as a whole in view, capitalism must ensure jobs and pay, so that there is not too large a 'reserve army' of unemployed to threaten the established order, and so that enough people earn enough money to buy the commodities produced. Massive unemployment is disturbing to the capitalist as well as to the worker. For the worker it threatens livelihood and the possibilities of a worthwhile life; for the capitalist it threatens mainly the ideological basis of his or her privileged position, but that is bad enough.

So the State in Australia provides both an employment service, the Commonwealth Employment Scheme (CES), to help willing workers to find jobs, and subsistence money, the dole, to unemployed people who have no other means of support and are not 'dole bludgers'. The two functions are administered by the same department, the Department of Social Security, but in different branches, expressing different components of the total message, the attitude of the State towards the unemployed. We will look at a number of key texts through which this complex meaning is articulated—especially for young unemployed, where the anomalous category of youth exacerbates the problem of ambiguous attitudes. This is partly because the State-as-parent must have special tenderness for the young, partly because the socialisation of the young is not yet complete and they constitute a threat if they are left outside the social body.

The journey of an unemployed youth through the CES system is itself a text as well as an encounter with other kinds of text; our unemployed youth is called Anna. Her first port of call is the CES office, which mediates the system to the unemployed who are its clients. CES offices are scattered round the cities of Australia, mainly in suburbs, especially working-class suburbs. They are typically embedded in the commercial life of those suburbs, in shopping centres or other groups of shops and offices. Normally the entrance is at the back of a building, literally a back door, with all the significance that has. The CES centre we visited was behind a bank. We passed through a glass door and turned left, down a corridor, at the end of which was a list of tenants of the building beside a lift. On the bottom floor (apart from the bank) we passed five dentists and a physiotherapist, on the way to the CES office occupying the whole of the second floor. If we had overshot we would have found, on the third floor, a plastic surgeon, an allergist, an occupational therapist, a gastro-enterologist, and the Anglican Parish office, and a few others.

We took the lift to the first floor, and went along a corridor to the glass doors of a large open-plan room, about 25 by 18 m. Diagonally opposite the door was a temporary desk, with a notice reading 'Enquiries' on it. Scattered round the room were four smaller, lower, free-standing desks. Along the wall to the left were five rooms partitioned off by bright red screens. The carpet was well worn, an undistinguished blue pattern. Piped music, instrumental, played quietly in the background. Behind the flimsy desks were clerks, standing, as were the clients (there are no chairs for them). All were relatively young and casually dressed—one wore no shoes, her bare feet easily visible behind the desk structure. The room decor was bare, in grave need of a paint job, but it was spacious, with extensive windows. The signifiers of power, of distance between staff and clients, were as minimal as they could be. When we visited there were four staff, and eight people waiting, and those people received unhurried attention. Anna was impressed by the attention she received. The person seeing her took her into one of the red rooms for a fuller discussion, focusing sympathetically on her problems with the previous job she had obtained through the CES. For Anna, the process took 26 minutes, with no waiting around, and this was apparently fairly normal.

The signifiers of the CES office and the experience carry a single message: benign powerlessness. The staff are approachable, concerned, friendly, but with limited help they can offer. The other two sites to visit are places of more real power.

One is the Job Centre. This runs independently of the CES. It is a much smaller room but more brightly furnished. When we entered, the sound of Don Henley's recent hit, 'Down at the Sunset Grill', could be heard. In the CES centre, notices thanked you for not smoking; here you could light up if you wanted to. The small

space was packed with display boards for job-notices, each carefully typed out on a card, organised in broad categories. Anna saw
two jobs that might suit. She followed the correct procedures, as
spelled out by a large notice: step 1, fill in a form complete with job
number; step 2, hand it in at the counter, and wait until your name
is called. The interview this time was more complex and demanding: this was for real. The clerk got the full job details from the
computer (fuller than the description card) and consulting this she
asked Anna details about her experience, to decide whether she was
suitable. If the clerk approves, she rings the employer to make an
appointment. Anna was left aware that she wasn't really trusted to
want to work: she has been judged twice, and found only half-
wanting. The distrust, of course, is realistic. Because the dole pay-
ment is tied to a 'genuine' wish to have a job, unemployed persons
are rightly suspected of wanting to have job applications on their
record, while not bothering to go through with the interview.

Finally there was a trip to the DSS office to apply for Social
Security benefits. There are fewer DSS offices than CES offices, and
they are associated strongly with other government agencies, rather
than shops or professional offices. The one we visited shared a
ground floor with the State Electricity Commission and the Water
Board. Above it was the Community Welfare Department, a children's court, a probation and parole board, and a registry of births,
marriages and deaths. The office itself was, like the CES office,
at the back of the building, but smaller and altogether better
appointed. It was a long narrow room, with a reception area containing groups of seats, and a series of seven individual numbered
desks along one wall, and five interview rooms along the other. The
seats were blue, nicely upholstered, but grouped in fours, two
chairs back to back, with rigid arms enclosing each individual. The
message of the chairs and the booths was clear: a person must be as
self-contained as possible, interacting with no one. A large notice
reinforced this:

> Proving who you are
> • Stops fraud
> • Protects your personal information

Whose fraud is stopped by this proof of who you are (surely not
the government defrauding the citizen?) or how this 'protects' your
personal information (and who from) wasn't made clear by the
notice, which simply contributed to a sense of vague paranoia

directed everywhere. While waiting for the interview one could read the 'No smoking' notice (as in the CES office) and make use of the ashtrays kindly provided (as in the Job Centre). The piped music was indistinguishable from the CES background sound, but there was a notice board here, with notices to read. On the day of our visit, the headings were as follows (reading from top to bottom, and from right to left): 'Legal problems? Apply for legal aid...'; 'Renting: tenants' information'; 'Spouse carer's pension'; 'Unemployed and aged between 15 and 24?'; 'Crisis care'; 'Volunteer task force'; 'Handicapped child's allowance'; 'Bar training scheme'.

Faced with this exhaustive choice of implied classifications of her self, Anna was strongly moved to apply for the bar training scheme. She felt the oppressive ideology of the place, the sense of loss of self-worth and isolation. She did not object to the rigid seats, back to back, though: for her that arrangement fitted exactly how she was feeling, desperately attempting to feel superior to the other failures in the room, or at least separate and different. The 'reserve army of the unemployed' is effectively coerced to see themselves as no army, just a set of people of no worth and no individuality. Anna would submit to this experience only for the money, but that made it no better. Once registered, she would not have to wait in this room each time, but every fortnight she would come in to the office and drop her form into a box provided to the left of the entrance: relatively swift and untaxing, but still alienating and privatised.

The 'text' we have looked at, typical as it is, is not specifically Australian and not 'culture' as that word is commonly understood. What is revealed is an ideological schema, a set of meanings and assumptions that are no less fundamental to Australian life for being so typical of capitalist-state bureaucracies. But this ideological schema shows fissures as well as strategies. The division of the CES and the DSS corresponding to different functions has its own effect, setting up a narrative, a rite of passage that the unemployed persons must perform with their own bodies, acting out their meaning. But this division also signals the contradictions between these functions. The CES office is the interface between the unemployed and the bureaucracy. It expresses identity with the unemployed, the State as a powerless but understanding friend. At the next stage of the progression, however, the Job Centre, the character of the unemployed person is split into potential employee/suspected delinquent, someone to be helped to get a job, but not

trusted to want one. Finally, at the DSS, there is another classification, again a double classification, as an innocent victim or cunning
manipulator of the system. There is now a loop, linking the DSS
and the Job Centre in a cycle, the cycle of the unemployed, oscillat-
ing between the two kinds of double message. The State is now
powerful but not helpful, knowledgeable about 'who you are' but
still suspicious and without real understanding. The unemployed
Anna is now part of the State, as information stored in a computer,
but no longer part of the social order isolated from those in work
because she is no longer like them, and from other unemployed
persons because she is.

Time on Their Hands: The Case of the Video Parlour

In this section we shall examine the concept of 'leisure' and its intrinsic connection to the concept of work. Leisure is, in contemporary usage, a kind of not-working, but a very different kind of
not-working to unemployment. The word comes from the Latin
licere, which is also the root of the word 'licence'. It means something that is permitted, within a set of duties or obligations. So
'leisure' is a circumscribed period when work is allowed to be
omitted. Without work, then, to frame its beginning and end,
leisure cannot exist. Precisely because unemployment is so dangerously like leisure, except that it lacks these firm boundaries,
leisure too becomes a problematic category—especially if the
unemployed have equal or greater access to its forms.

Leisure and work are an intrinsically related pair of categories,
but they aren't equal or symmetrical. Leisure activities are in fact
formed by their relation to work, and not vice versa. We will illus-
trate with just one leisure activity which is currently very popular
in Australia, especially among young unemployed males: video
games, in amusement parlours. (For a fuller analysis of video parlours from which much of our discussion derives, see Fiske &
Watts, 1985.) Like so many forms of popular culture, video parlours provoke polarised responses. 'The West Australian Premier
has said that he would like to take an axe to them . . . but President
Reagan thinks they are terrific,' reported *The West Australian* on 2
May 1983. Almost two years later to the day, Premier Burke was
handed an axe, in the form of the legal judgment that video games
contravened laws relating to the use of gambling machines. Far

from using this gratuitous axe, the government moved as swiftly as possible to allay the fears of amusement parlour owners. The about-face is an especially clear signal that this form of leisure is not after all seen as a subversive force, and that criticism of it is just a rhetorical move, a symbolic act which must remain at that level.

In our journey through this cultural site we were guided this time by Chris, not Anna (girls are less likely to play video games, as both agreed). The siting of the video games we are looking at is important. Video games for home-use are common, but the ones that concern us are in the video parlours. The video parlour is a shop, but what it lacks that shops reassuringly offer is a clearly marked entrance, and a service counter to signal the cash nexus which links customer to seller. What we see is a shabbily carpeted tunnel, with rows of machines along each wall, almost a parody of the DSS office with its rows of individual booths. Both are in a sense transformations of the workplace in one of its most alienating forms, the assembly-line. In *Empire of Signs* Roland Barthes provides a powerful description of pachinko (a Japanese equivalent of pinball) which points in this direction:

> The pachinko is a collective and solitary game. The machines are set up in long rows; each player standing in front of his panel plays for himself, without looking at his neighbor, whom he nonetheless brushes with his elbow . . . the parlour is a hive, a factory—the players seem to be working on an assembly line. The imperious meaning of the scene is that of a deliberate, absorbing labour. [pp. 27–8]

Pachinko differs from video games in that the player can win the silver balls necessary to play it. These may be used for more games, or exchanged for small prizes. Barthes continues:

> Here we understand the seriousness of a game which counters constipated parsimony of salaries, the constriction of capitalist wealth, with the voluptuous debacle of silver balls, which, all of a sudden, fill the player's hand. [p. 29]

Pachinko wasn't one of the games on offer in the video parlour we entered, and in spite of the overall similarities, the differences have cultural importance. The Japanese game appears to be played mainly by adult workers and provides them with signifiers of money and commodities as the reward for skill. This is ideologically very different from video games, which seem to offer no rewards at all, a difference that must say something about the different kind of players, and their different relationship to economic and work processes.

A major point of the games in this arcade is simply to resist paying money. In our investigation we met many games players (including Chris) who told us of their immense satisfaction at making 20 or 40 cents last 'for hours'. There was a common tendency to boast about (and perhaps exaggerate) the length of time that the player could deny the machine its next coin. Frequently, players are consciously aware that in resisting the machine they are asserting their interests against those of the owner. The longer their 20 cents last, the greater their pleasure at 'beating the system', in the all encompassing sense that phrase has in the common speech.

Not putting more coins in the slot, the pleasure of not paying for pleasure in a society that has made leisure into a consumer industry, is in fact a subversion of the nexus that normally links work and leisure in the dominant economic order. In that order leisure serves work, because workers submit to the work discipline in order to have money to enjoy leisure through the commodities that make leisure enjoyable. And production of commodities for leisure use in turn provides employment, and profits, in a benign cycle that keeps workers happily in work, and capitalists in pocket. What the video player is doing is in effect to short-circuit this cycle by working in a leisure situation. He works not with the machine but against it. The better the machinist is, the less he pays, and the lower the profit of the owner. This inverts the basic logic of capitalism, where the skill and speed of the machinist is meant to increase not decrease the profits of the owner. The machine consumes instead of producing, and the machinist pays instead of being paid. If the money used, and saved, in this way comes from the dole, the triumph over the system is so much the greater.

The way in which the video game uses the logic of capitalism is to subvert it. Under capitalism, the commodity the worker sells is labour-power, measured in units of time. Connected to this is a widespread conception of time as money, and both as commodities which should be 'saved' not 'wasted'. The video game operates with this potent equation to attack its fundamental terms. The machine declares the connection between time and money, but for the good player to save money requires a waste of time. Only for the inexpert does the ideological bond hold, so that time and money are both wasted at a common rate, with nothing else produced or consumed.

But ideological games like this aren't the primary motive for the games player. For Chris, the pleasure of the game is his sense of achievement, measured in absolutely objective terms as a score remembered by the machine and repeated to other competitors as the score to beat. As a temporarily unemployed bricklayer, who left school at 15, Chris doesn't have too many other achievements that are so clear cut. From his skill at various games he gains a sense of identity and a sense of being in control—two experiences that are conspicuously lacking from his life whether he is employed or not.

The sense of being in control is of course ultimately illusory, since the machine's ultimate triumph is guaranteed by its inexorable program. But the need for this illusion is strong, especially among working-class youths. Paul Willis, writing in *Culture, Ideology and Social Process*, reports the same phenomenon among working-class youths in Britain:

> Another main theme of working class culture—at least as I observed it in the manufacturing industries of the Midlands—is the massive attempt to gain informal control of the work process.

He goes on to link this adult behaviour in the work place with the behaviour of working-class children in a school setting:

> Again this is effectively mirrored for us by working class kids' attempts, with the aid of resources of their culture, to take control of classes, substitute their own unofficial timetables, and control their own routines and life spaces. [p. 83]

Although Willis is talking about Britain not Australia, the same forces and the same responses to a common experience of alienation are at issue. But the working-class culture in the factory and the alternative culture in the school, as described by him, are direct if covert actions on the system itself. The video game expresses the same meanings, but only at a symbolic level. That is why it can be seen, by a President Reagan and perhaps even a Premier Burke, as an instrument of social control rather than a force of resistance. It could only become that if the games-players could sustain their sense of self-worth outside the video arcade and seek an equivalent sense of control over the work place or the school room or the DSS office.

This sense of control also contrasts video games with television. Chris doesn't watch television much. If he watches anything it's usually a video film chosen by him or others in his group.

Underlying this preference is his need to be in control. With videos he can choose what narrative to consume, but then must submit to the unfolding of the narrative, with group interaction the only means of resistance. But with video games he is to some degree in control of the narrative itself as its author and hero. In practice Chris's main aim is a high score, irrespective of narrative virtuosity. He could, however, hasten the inevitable end or affect the way it occurs, playing safe or manufacturing risks.

Chris's reasons for preferring video games to TV are probably widespread, and not confined to Australian players. Patricia Greenfield in *Mind and Media* reported on American children who preferred video games over TV:

> They were . . . unanimous about the reason: active control. The meaning of control was both very concrete and very conscious. One nine-year-old girl said, 'In TV if you want to make someone die, you can't. In Pac-Man, if you want to run into a ghost you can.' Another girl of the same age said, 'On TV you can't say "shoot now" or, with Popeye, "eat your spinach now".' She went on to say she would get frustrated sometimes watching Popeye and wanting him to eat his spinach at a certain time when he didn't. [p. 91]

But the power of the games player as author is strictly limited. Although there are more varied games, such as 'Dragon's Lair', which offer the full gamut of narrative choices—from tragic failure, to heroic and romantic success—most games have more or less complicated versions of winning and losing: the inevitability of ultimate defeat is clearly recognised. This totally predictable and inescapable outcome ought to induce a sense of fatalism, though Chris gives no signs of this after a good game. Indeed, the involuntary muscular spasm which is a frequent reaction to a player's final 'dent' is a complex mixture of despair, release from concentration and elation.

A final contradiction associated with video parlours concerns the issue of resistance versus conformity. When a political leader, say, a premier, threatens to take an axe to something we would assume that that something is a serious threat to the social order, unless the premier is only joking. There are signifiers of resistance, as we've seen, but that resistance is highly controlled and operates by way of many of the basic terms and values of capitalism, even if in inverse form. Everyone we saw in a video parlour seemed to be concentrat-

Great escape from pressure

SURFBOARD riding is the rock 'n roll sport of the world.

From the Beach Boys of the 60s, through psychedelic Flower Power, The Stomp, Heavy Metal and Punk, the two life-styles have always · been closely aligned in fashion and philosophy.

SURFING

with Peter Boyle

Triggs Point surfer Greg Green is one man who has managed to fuse his passion for both into a high-voltage career.

Greenie, as he is known on the beach, manages the nationally-known Perth rock 'n roll band, The Frames.

Along with lead singer Dean Denton and hard-driving electric base player Mark Donohue, Green escapes from the pressures of business promotion, hotel gigs and recording contracts to the world of wetsuits and tri-fin thruster surfboards whenever possible.

During a recent visit to Victoria Greg and the boys managed to slip away from Melbourne for a day's surfing at Bells Beach with Rod Brooks, owner of Piping Hot Wetsuits and one of the band's national sponsors.

"Often after a heavy working night we need a real mind-cleansing, heart-starter to get going the next day," said Green.

Outrageous

"Nothing works better for us than a crisp session in the waves."

This Wednesday, June 26 at 8pm, The Frames perform at the Scimitar Boardriders' Club annual P Party at the Castle Hotel, North Beach.

Open to the general public, the P Party is four hours of outrageous rock-n-roll fun, with one major requirement — everyone has to wear fancy dress in a costume beginning with the letter P.

Tickets are available at Cordingley Surf City, 201 West Coast Highway, Scarborough Beach for $3 per person or at the door on Wednesday night for $4.

'The Frames' link three domains of youth culture, surfing, rock 'n' roll and pubs, and the pleasures of each are the sensual ones of the body which allow it to resist or oppose social control. But Peter Boyle's real theme is their ambiguous relationship with work. Greenie makes money out of the link, and he makes it in pubs. The example of a 'great escape' in Victoria is a day's surfing with Rod Brooks, one of the band's national sponsors. Rock is part of a 'heavy working night', a hangover which the surf dispels: nothing 'works' better. Peter Boyle celebrates not surfing, music or pubs, but the success of commercial motives in incorporating these subversive elements back into the social world, justifying the 'politics of pleasure' as good business sense.

ing intensely and not obviously likely to cause an affray. This judgment seems to be in line with police views. The South Australian
police commissioned a study which found no evidence to link video
arcades with behavioural problems. Western Australian police are
reported as not being worried by arcades in WA (*Western Mail*, 2
June 1983).

The plot content of most of the games is also conformist. The
games build a polarised structure, an 'us' versus 'them', and they
position a player precisely: only 'us' can play. In the game the fleets
of 'them' are inexhaustible, pouring from the heart of the program
to their ultimate overwhelming victory over the lone human de-
fender. In no game that we have heard of are the enclosures specific or
political: images of President Reagan or Margaret Thatcher cannot
be blasted from the skies, much less Fraser, Whitlam, Hawke or
Howard. No cartoon figures of bloated capitalists, no school prin-
cipals or senior police appear as monsters to be avoided or zapped.
Rather the enemies are anonymous and robotic, or electronic versions of traditional monsters, ghosts or insects. It's possible to
reflect that these faceless forces of the enemy in fact proceed from
computers which are a symbol of capitalist technology, their re-
morseless onslaught drawing on the alienated energies of human
beings. However, we saw no signs of such a reflection dawning on
the faces of the dedicated players.

Rather, there is rejection of meanings as the player reduces
himself to a physical response—as the pleasures of surfing and of
rock are the pleasures of the body, so too is the pleasure of video
games. In all three aspects of youth culture, the concentration on
the physical senses is a way of resisting social control, a way of
celebrating the physical existence of youth that momentarily frees
the young man from the pressures of social control and gives him
the pleasure of living in that over which he has control (his body)
rather than in that over which he is powerless (society). (As we saw
in the first chapter, Nietzsche found a similar subversive meaning
in Dionysiac drunkenness.)

We use the masculine gender here deliberately because surfing
and video parlours are particularly male pleasures; rock is enjoyed
equally by females, despite the masculinity of much of its lyrics,
music and players. Surfing and video games emphasise physical
skill and control, and this is particularly appealing to young males
with little social power. The reason for this is not hard to find. Our
culture constructs masculinity so that its meanings are expressed in

dominance, power over others and social control. But it then denies the subordinate male the means to exercise this dominance by denying him access to any form of social power. Thus the ranks of surfers and video players contain disproportionately large numbers of the unemployed, truanting school students, social 'drop outs' and other young males who know they are not going to 'make it' through the socially validated channels of a good job and/or a good education.

For girls, the social pressures towards dominance and control are fewer and weaker in our culture, though this is changing. Rock music may be more important for girls for two reasons. The first is that it deals with sexuality—that is, with relations between the sexes, rather than the gender specific masculinity of surfing and video games. Admittedly this sexuality is male dominated, but then so is the public world that the adolescent girl inhabits, and, as English cultural theorist Angela McRobbie has shown, she often has to retire to the privacy of her or her friend's bedroom to find a space for a female youth subculture. The second is that rock music is associated with dance and styles of dress and make-up by which the young girl can express a social identity through display and, in so doing, express a female identity within a male culture. McRobbie has also shown that for girls the sexual movements of dance are often autoerotic; that is, they are the means by which girls can enjoy the sexuality of their own bodies for themselves, and not through the eyes of, or for the satisfaction of, males. These opportunities are not offered so readily by video arcades or surfing, though sunbaking on the beach can be seen as an important part of female culture and display, which also contains elements of health autoeroticism.

American companies dominate the video game market, and so specific Australian inflections are rare, and this absence is significant. The games make no attempt to construct a national identity, outside this vague membership of an 'us', and this has the effect of assimilating Australian video players into an American mega-self.

For all these reasons, it's not possible now to claim that video parlours are either distinctively Australian or a focus of critical, oppositional thinking and feeling among the young working-class and unemployed. Yet they are already part of Australian culture in an equally important, non-exclusive sense, as much an integral aspect of current ways of thinking and feeling and meaning as more uniquely Australian cultural forms. They provide a space within which a sense of opposition can be expressed and made into both pleasure and a sense of achievement or self-worth. This function, in the subculture of the unemployed and other subordinate groups, may be seen as helping them to cope with their position and its contradictions and thus helps to act as a panacea. But it would be facile to dismiss the critical potential of this activity and the way that its meanings work within the strategies of domination and subordination, of power and resistance, that characterise the cultural polities of capitalism.

TV and the World of School

Work and school are two major sites where social control is exercised on younger and older Australians. Each is locked into the other, because school is the specific work of the young; as they produce themselves or are produced as commodities for the labour market, it is the place where they are graded and socialised for different roles in the work force. Leisure, then, is equally the absence of one or the other kind of work. Players of video games are as likely to be truants from school as unemployed. There are many other leisure activities, but pre-eminent among them in contemporary Australia is TV watching. This is quintessentially a 'leisure' activity, to be engaged in only outside school and work hours. As such, it is obviously a central component of popular culture. In this section we don't want to address the whole field of Australian TV in any comprehensive way. That is itself a topic for a book, and many books have been written on it. What we want to do instead is to look at one particular issue, the refractions of the world of work and of school in some Australian TV programs, and through this, suggest some of the complex ways in which mass culture, as packaged by the media industry, is articulated with the common or popular culture as it is lived by millions of ordinary Australians.

The program type we will start with is the quiz show. (The discussion here is drawn substantially from John Fiske's 1982 article on quiz shows, and Hodge and Tripp's *Children and Television*, both listed in our bibliography.) The basic concept for quiz shows was borrowed from abroad, but they have become quickly naturalised. Australian-produced quiz shows were among the first Australian programs to figure in the ten top-rating programs. They are especially popular with children, but they justify possession of prime-time slots by their capacity to attract a large aggregate family audience. Their popularity, then, is not in doubt: but what exactly are they saying?

As a start to an answer, here is an exchange between an educationist (Tripp) and a thirteen-year-old school boy (Ashley) talking about the use of school knowledge:

Tripp: What, um. . . , is any of it any use to you? To learn all that stuff? [The Industrial Revolution]

Ashley: Yeah . . . say if you want to be a teacher or something.

Tripp: Yeah, but do you want to be a teacher?

Ashley: No.

Tripp: No? What would you want to do?

Ashley: Welding and . . .

Tripp: Do you? Well, what's the good of learning all about how factories used to be, or what they used before the seed drill was invented or something, if you want to weld?

Ashley: Don't know . . . just . . . have to go there [school] don't we?

Tripp: Right . . . um . . . does it make any difference whether you learn it or not?

Ashley: Yeah.

Tripp: Does it? What sort of difference does it make?

Ashley: Um . . . don't know . . . um . . . if we . . . like . . . you have to know all the things if you go on 'Sale of the Century', or something like that.

Tripp: Right.

Ashley: If you don't go to school you're not going to win that are you?

Tripp: You're not going to . . .

Ashley: Win the thing are you?

Ashley here is confronting and resolving the problematic relationship between work and school on which the legitimacy of the education system is based. The history of work as a relevant curriculum content is offered by Tripp but rejected by Ashley. Its relevance for his specific prospective job as a welder is also far from clear. In practice, the connection between work and school knowledge is far more abstract than this. The ideology that sustains the school system makes a long-term connection between work at school and ultimate rewards. The logic is a double-chain, of the following form:

$$\begin{array}{ccccc}
\text{effort} & \text{school} & & \text{wealth} + \\
+ \text{ ability} & \rightarrow \text{success} \rightarrow & \text{good jobs} & \rightarrow & \text{commodities}
\end{array}$$

$$\begin{array}{cccc}
\text{lack of effort} & \text{school} & \text{poor jobs,} & \text{poverty} + \\
+ \text{ lack of ability} \rightarrow & \text{failure} \rightarrow & \text{unemployment} \rightarrow & \text{no commodities}
\end{array}$$

This double chain has a double function. It legitimates school and effort at school, and it justifies a society in which wealth and opportunity are not distributed equally. It provides an alternative explanation for this inequality, based on lack of innate abilities, plus culpable laziness at a crucial period of life, rather than an explanation in terms of built-in privileges along class lines.

For Ashley, the completion of this chain in endlessly deferred, so he offers instead a shorter chain, in which quiz shows play a crucial role. In his version, school knowledge, plus luck, leads straight into success in the great test (e.g. *Sale of the Century*), with a bonanza of prizes that can be savoured every night of the school week. This may not be a realistic series of expectations, and he may well admit that, but it is the only possible vindication of school knowledge for him. However, it is a vindication at some cost. The world of work is eliminated from the chain. As Altman (like the rest of us) has suggested, Ashley is constructed as a potential consumer, not a potential worker. So the quiz show resolves the problem of the relation between school and work by magically eliminating the need for work. The prizes appear in abundant profusion, courtesy of well-known brand names with not a greasy hand holding a spanner to be seen, and the well-dressed competitors carry them off without any signs of effort beyond what is required to press a button. In such a show, work is literally obscene (the word comes from Latin, meaning 'what should not be shown on stage').

Quiz shows don't attempt to reproduce the whole of school. School is signified by a single function, the function of the test. Public examinations are the most dramatic symbol of that function, but they are too impersonal and negative to be a suitable image for this ideological purpose, though some quiz shows—Mastermind, for instance—do in fact come close to it. The staple quiz show approximates more to the test as it is embedded in normal classroom discourse, mystified in the interaction which teachers and pupils engage in. We can bring out the parallels by a description of the central activity of the quiz show. The quiz master (teacher) tells the competitors (pupils) what to do, how and when: this is a highly

'The Sale of the Century'

THE 'KNOWLEDGE'

THE EXAMINER

THE CANDIDATES

THE INSTANT REWARD

But where is work?

rule-governed form of activity, and the meticulous observance of these rules is an important part of the 'hidden curriculum', as it has been called, of both schools and quiz games. The quizmaster, like the teacher, works in total harmony with unseen experts; in quiz shows they are more visible than at school and are occasionally revealed on camera, with headphones on and technology at their fingertips. The competitors sit in a row and generally have to answer as individuals, though sometimes they can break off into small discussion groups and function as a team (as in 'progressive' classrooms). The questions are a peculiar kind of question, found mainly in quiz shows and classrooms. They are pseudo-questions, in that the quizmaster/teacher knows the answers before the questions are posed and does not want to know the answers personally, only whether the competitors know them. Such questions are also found in the regimes of religious instruction, in the catechism, and they carry many of the ideological structures of that traditional domain into these secular forms. The catechism-form turns problems of faith into items of knowledge. The questions involved are either factual or treated as factual, with no dispute about what is a right or wrong answer. There is one common variation, in both schools and quiz games: the 'guess-what-I'm-thinking' sequences so beloved of teachers, where the clues are released gradually and the first competitor/pupil to guess and complete the utterance successfully wins.

The parallels are not perfect, of course. The quizmaster is a more pleasant version of the teacher, and the assumption of superiority which determines teacher–student relations is displaced on to the headphoned expert who composed the questions. Most quizmasters indicate their mastery of the *game*, not the knowledge, and foreground the skill of the players playing it in the first place. ('He's fast, isn't he?', Tony Barber will say of a contestant, referring to the speed with which he or she presses the buzzer, rather than the process of intellection that allows them to do it at all.) The tendency to refer to winners as 'the champ' inserts sporting discourse into the contest, making the fight between contestants as much one of 'natural' talent as of learning and education. The aim of the quizmaster is to provide a 'good game', a 'close contest'—sport—and this reduces knowledge to simply the raw material for the spectacle of the game itself.

There are class relationships built into the various quiz shows which also affect the nature of their relationship to school knowledge. At one class extreme, the BBC format *Mastermind* is very close to official school knowledge, but it is not one of the most popular shows. A quick look at its audience and at its contestants establishes this as a show for people who were good at school and maybe teach in one now. Its questions are arcane and make use of the contestants' own 'special interests'—their reusing of the skills taught them in school and their intrinsic interest in learning. The structure is explicitly that of the examination—the headmasterly inquisitor, with the time limit on answer periods—or the interrogation—the spotlit chair and the almost comically formal demeanour of the quizmaster and the contestants. The kind of knowledge learned at school is kid's stuff for this program, and few at home could participate in the way assumed to be the case for *Sale of the Century*. It demonstrates the link between education and jobs as well as education and privilege, and an analysis of the occupations of *Mastermind* contestants and those of *Sale of the Century* contestants would no doubt reveal this. Finally, *Mastermind*'s reward for success is not a lavish supply of consumer goods, but an object of antiquity or high art associations; the test has been passed, and a small cachet of the elite is the prize.

Sale of the Century is more down-market than this and asks questions that could well have been in our school curriculum. Its prizes link success in education directly with consumer goods, although not necessarily the most useful ones; the top prize is a pair of BMW cars whose value is more of display than utility despite the invocations of German efficiency. Some popular shows actually subvert school curricula and official education. *The New Price is Right* demotes educational knowledge in favour of the expertise of the housewife in her role as expert consumer and budgeter, her 'work' being to spend with precision the money earned by someone else in another place. In this show, the emphasis is on egalitarianism, luck, and the participation of the audience in offering advice to the predominantly female contestants. The games played within the show draw on physical skills as well, such as putting a golf ball, or running around a string of objects and placing prices on them as quickly as possible. Its prizes, too, tend to be useful whitegoods, and home decorating and handyman goods, rather than leisure goods. The car offered, too, is the more proletarian family sedan—a Bluebird or a Subaru, for instance.

It is hard to see *The New Price is Right*'s subversion of school knowledge as radical in any sense, but that claim is more plausible in relation to a show such as *Family Feud*. In that show, a choice of answers is given and the contestant must arrange them in order of popularity. The points you accumulate in this way are, in effect, aggregations of the population who agree with you, and you are rewarded for maximum incorporation into the social consensus. Here, typically, representativeness is what is rewarded, and even if the common response is incorrect or ignorant, as is sometimes the case, the contestants are rewarded for sharing the limitations of their peers. In *Family Feud* there is no such thing as official knowledge, only common practice. Researchers, Mills and Rice have put the interesting case that this format is a new and potentially radical form of quiz show because it takes the final authority from the dominant quizmaster (with behind him the dictionary or encyclopaedia) and gives it over to 'us', the typical citizen. This shift is by no means complete. 'Us' is a sample of 100 people, chosen by the program makers on grounds that are not revealed, and it promotes the survey method as the new secular form of reading oracles. Yet the difference undoubtedly exists, as an ideological message repeated with every program, read and affirmed by millions of viewers. It's important to recognise that even within one genre of TV there is difference and contradiction which offer the possibility of different meanings in the culture for different categories of people.

Despite such class and ideological differences, most quiz shows to some degree seem to affirm the values of the education system and a consumer society. To many parents, quiz shows are 'educational' and therefore something the kids could be encouraged to watch. This is one of the benefits of TV in common wisdom, its educative function. Yet, TV's relation to education is not always as clearly and directly constructed as it is in quiz shows. A soap opera that was very popular with school children, particularly in its early days, was *Prisoner*. Far from being educational, this program was deplored by educationists, and its popularity with children seen to be the source of alarm. As we shall see, this alarm may have expressed itself in ways that missed the special interest *Prisoner* has for school children, but it was accurate in its sense that any connection between *Prisoner* and school was not likely to be a benevolent one. *Prisoner* does have a relation to school and connects closely with quiz shows in its occupation of an oppositional space in its interrogation of both school and work.

Prisoner is set in a women's prison. Schools are not literally prisons, but prisons are a powerful metaphor for schools and children. *Children and Television* tells how David Tripp found, with three classes of children aged eleven to thirteen, that there was overwhelming agreement that schools are like prisons. The children produced the following list of similarities:

1. Pupils are shut in.
2. Pupils are separated from their friends.
3. Pupils would not be there if they were not made to be.
4. Pupils only work because they are punished and it's less boring than doing nothing at all.
5. Pupils have no rights: they cannot do anything about an unfair teacher.
6. Some teachers victimise pupils.
7. There are gangs and leaders amongst the pupils.
8. There are silly rules which everyone tries to break.

This list shows clearly the point of contact between school and prison, for children, and the kind of issues that can be explored through this kind of program. Where quiz shows focus on knowledge as a commodity linked to other commodities, underpinned by an all-pervasive and unquestioned set of social rules, *Prisoner* focuses on the operation of power, the imposition of rules by social agents who are good and bad, but mostly indifferent, and it takes the position of subordinates who accept the regime reluctantly at best. In this way, *Prisoner* could be seen to adopt a critical perspective, explicitly from outside the social consensus. It mobilises children's experience of the operation of power in schools, and so the connection it makes with the world of work is itself potentially critical. Alternatively, its linking the world of work, and the working class, with the criminal could be seen as a reactionary assertion of the legitimacy of their economic subordination.

In *Prisoner* the adult female prisoners are not at school. What they are more often engaged in is work that is crushingly trivial and unproductive: scrubbing floors, picking up litter, working in the laundry. This is work that the immates do because they are required to do it, not because they choose or want to, or could get any satisfaction in doing it. It is a strong metaphor for children's activities in school. It's not a metaphor for work itself, however, but an actual foretaste. So where quiz shows jump over work to connect school with a set of rewards for achievement, *Prisoner* presents work and adult experience as continuous with school, equally boring, pointless and alienating. The unpleasant aspects of school (prison) won't be compensated for later by a rich and satisfying afterlife as worker or consumer. It will be simply more of the same, so the strategies for survival and resistance developed in school will be just as useful afterwards. The grim message received by the young viewers of *Prisoner* is that the domination they endure at school is replicated by other structures outside it—it is not a training ground in the sense that they will enter a different world on graduating. The recognition of this is threatening to the school, but it probably assists society in its insistence on the pervasiveness of mechanisms of social control.

Schools as ideological sites transmit a set of meta-messages, preparing pupils for their later role in various parts of the socio-economic order, and justifying the rightness of that order. But practices of resistance emerge among subordinate groups, and as Willis (whom we quoted earlier in this chapter) argues, this happens among working-class children in Britain. He makes a link between the working-class culture in school and 'shop-floor culture' in factories. The same process, we have been arguing, occurs in

Australian society and culture. The overall culture is far from homogeneous. It includes the cultural forms of the CES and DSS, emanating from the government, so powerfully coercive that if there are forms of resistance we were unable to detect them on those actual sites. It includes phenomena such as video arcades, where technology is both celebrated and used as an inversion of the dominant order, keeping youths from gainful work as it develops their unproductive skills and sense of confidence and control. It is also packaged and sold by media organisations for mass consumption, but even at this level we can see contradiction and struggle between dominant ideological forms and alternative, oppositional forms. So the balance is different in different genres, in different programs, even in different individual shows.

Overall, the dominance of the dominant is usually put into question, just as resistance is typically contained and channelled and neutralised by a variety of means. But even more important than a recognition of the complexity of cultural forms is the realisation that cultural meanings cannot be interpreted solely from the study of texts. We can't decide whether *Prisoner* or *Family Feud* or video arcades are ultimately on the side of the dominant order simply by counting up conformist elements in one column and critical elements in another. What matters is how these meanings are integrated into a way of life of individuals and groups, as part of their social existence. That can change and thereby transform the meaning of a social form for a specific group. Underlying shifts and contradictions in these cultural forms, however, there is a structural source which is not likely to change quickly while Australia is a capitalist society: the pivotal yet ambiguous place of work in Australian life. It is the producer of wealth and leisure, yet it is invisible in the representation of wealth and leisure. It is both the source of economic value yet is itself disvalued, so that although it seems to exist for the sake of leisure, it gives leisure its specific forms and functions. Work is seen as a dehumanising grind, yet its absence is the supreme deprivation. This double meaning of work comes from the clash of interests, between those who do it and those who profit from it. It is only if we go to this level that we can make coherent sense of the myriad different forms work takes in the culture, as absence or presence, direct or transformed. So lack of work is as unthinkable at the CES as work is unspeakable in popular TV, yet they are all parts of a single society, a single culture.

5 Shopping

Buying, Leisure and Work

The need to deal with the problem of work is not, of course, confined to the unemployed or to those about to enter the employment market. Nor is work only that which earns a wage; the woman who is confined to 'home duties' is as much determined by her labour as the man who works in a factory. Video games or surfing, the pleasures of the body we have linked with youth, may offer some resistance to the constrictions and dehumanising effects of work. For the majority of our society, however, one of the main interventions in the attempt to define oneself in terms other than those provided by one's occupation occurs in the shopping centre. Shopping as a cultural practice is the subject of this chapter; its texts are the city shopping arcades such as Sydney's Centrepoint and Perth's Carillon Centre and the suburban shopping town or shopping centre, such as Sydney's Roselands, Melbourne's Chadstone or Perth's Carousel.

In an industrial, market-oriented society, buying is the essential correlative of producing, and leisure is the necessary opposite of work. The world of work is increasingly alienating and dehumanising; as the jobs get more and more repetitive and as the organisational control over them gets tighter and tighter, the more important leisure becomes for our development of a sense of identity in a world whose official working patterns seem to deny any such thing. Studies of people in the workplace show how constantly workers try to resist the control imposed upon them by the way that work is organised and by the technical demands of the machines they work with (or should it be for?). Inserting bits of behaviour that are decided by the worker and not by the machine or organisation can be seen as ways of asserting an identity and an individuality against the

95

depersonalising repetition demanded by so much work in the factory, the office or the home. This resistance to being defined as a cog in a machine is particularly strong in Australia with our myth, even an ideal, of the self-sufficient individual. The contradiction between a widely accepted ideal and widely spread working patterns creates a tension that the leisure industry exploits and attempts to resolve. In our leisure we do what we choose, at work we do what is demanded of us; what we do, and the conditions under which we do it, are important ways of constructing for ourselves both a personal and a social identity. Shopping finds its place within this context, and it has moved a long way from the purchase of essentials: it has become part of the leisure industry, and the commodities we buy are agents of pleasure and identity.

As we saw in our discussion of the suburban home, commodities are used to construct identity. The apparently immense choice the city shopping centres offer is less a choice between commodities for the buyer and more a choice of individual and social identity: the latent product of these centres. And just as the choice of commodity exists within clearly defined boundaries—ones set by fashion, taste, money and class—so the individualities on offer exist within similar defining limits. When Sydney's Centrepoint claims it 'ignites your passion for fashion' (their advertising slogan following the refurbishment in 1984) or exhorts you to be 'haute-coutured, coiffured, accessorised' (publicity leaflet) it is inviting you to come in and find a new you, a search that must be successful somewhere within 'three of the most fashion and trend-packed levels of shopping you'll find anywhere'.

The Pleasure of Looking

The act of going shopping is not simple, but a combination of a number of apparently different activities. Shopping is a spectacle in which one is both performer and spectator; it is browsing for the image or images that suit the personal taste; it is seeing and being seen, meeting and being met, a way of interacting with others. It is a functional activity, concerned with the acquisition of material goods, and a cultural one, concerned with the generation of personal and social identity and meanings. It is obviously in the interests of commerce to bring the two activities together as much as possible, and the whole strategy of the fashion industry is designed to do

Shopping, identity and the look

Browsing: literally, eating casually round a meadow looking for the grass or herbs that suit the taste. Here, looking for the image that fits the taste.

Spectacle–spectator. Shopping is entertainment, leisure, watching, listening, relaxing. The pleasures of the senses, the indulgence of the body, create the sense of the individual identity.

See and be seen, meet and be met. Identity comes from interacting with others. Images need spectators; lookers need spectacles (to look at and through).

this. But the commercial interests cannot, and do not, dominate our use of shopping centres completely. The interests of the shopper are also met, and the shopper can and does use these centres for (predominantly) her own motives rather than those of commerce; the manageress of a middle-range boutique in Centrepoint selling largely T-shirts, blouses and skirts priced between $15 and $40 estimated that she had 30–40 browsers in the shop for everyone who made a purchase. This is a high estimate; the lowest estimate given was 10–15 browsers for every purchase; the commonest, 20–25. But the point is clear: 'shopping' may or may not turn into sales, but it certainly meets the needs of the consumer.

The large city shopping centres, particularly, are designed for the window-shopper, the looker:

> It would be surprising to discover anyone who couldn't find what they were looking for in Carillon. But the most appealing feature of fashion buying Carillon-style is the atmosphere. There's no uncomfortable pressure to buy or hurry. In fact one can browse for hours on end.
>
> (advertisement for Perth's Carillon centre)

The most distinctive physical features of these centres are glass, light and reflective surfaces. Window-shopping is a stroll through a hall of mirrors. The plethora of light and reflection is designed not just to give a general impression of sparkle, plenitude, which seems to endow commodities with a magical inner life of their own; but, more importantly, it is designed to enhance the power and pleasure of looking. We must also remember that the obverse side of looking is being looked at: seeing implies being seen. Most city and suburban shopping centres facilitate this. There are balconies and viewing hatches for people to lean on and watch the spectacle below. Shoppers, particularly on late shopping nights, tend to dress up, knowing they will be looked at, deriving as much pleasure from displaying themselves as from looking at others.

Some shoppers are remarkably explicit and self-aware about this aspect, as the following comments made during interviews demonstrate:

> A: Yes, well you've got to look good here because I like looking at other people, you know, what they're wearing and ... er ... what I'm wearing.
>
> INTERVIEWER: So you enjoy people seeing you looking good?
>
> A: Oh yes, definitely ... [secretary, mid-twenties]

B: I come here with a few friends, you know, and we hang around, and have a look around, and things like that.

INTERVIEWER: Do you buy anything?

B: Oh no, not got the money (laughs) well, sometimes...

INTERVIEWER: What do you look at most, the shops or the people?

B: Oh both, really, see how they're dressed, you know, who they're with...

INTERVIEWER: Do you get dressed up specially to come here?

B: A bit [laughs] if I've got anything new, you know, show my friends... [School girl, year 10]

Both these interviewees were females, and that is no coincidence for these centres have an overwhelmingly female clientele. This is probably because our culture places so much emphasis on a woman's appearance as an indicator and constructor of her identity, and also because women are conditioned to be objects of the gaze; they are to be looked at by men. As John Berger has put it in *Ways of Seeing*, every woman in our society must constantly be the bearer of her own image; her identity is produced by people looking at her. No matter how narcissistic her motives initially, the woman constructing her ideal self from the commodities on offer appears to be constructing that self for the voyeurist pleasures of the male gaze. The 'self' she constructs, according to this theory, defines the class and type of man she is competing with other women to attract by the 'look', in both the word's senses—as an image and as a gaze. Throughout shopping centres the mirrors and the reflective surfaces enable the image and the gaze to become one.

There have been a number of theoretical inquiries into the act of looking as one of possession, whose findings may be helpful here. They are particularly useful as we examine the idea that we might construct our social and personal identities through various kinds of image—as the selection of clothes, for instance, can be seen to do for the shopper. The idea that our identity is formed by our 'image' seems at first sight to contain a charge of superficiality and shallowness, but this is only a first impression based partly upon the commonsense usage of the word 'image': to refer to an appearance designed to appeal rather than to tell the truth about what lies beneath it. An image, in this usage, tends to disguise reality, not convey it. This belief is based upon a misunderstanding of the way that language in general, and images and symbols in particular, actually work. The world is not composed of meaningful entities to which language attaches names or to which images refer. Neither products nor people have inner cores of meaning or self-definition that exist before and independently of their appearance, behaviour, use and social interaction. Rather, language and image help to construct the real and the meanings that we derive from it, which is to say the sense we make of it. They stand in an active and creative rather than a passive and reflective, relationship to the real. Image and style are not just means of self-expression, but of self-construction, and this self is constructed partly from and by the look.

Freud and, after him, Lacan, have devoted much of their analysis of our behaviour to attempting to explain the pleasure of looking. For Freud it was bound up with possession and power. The small child, looking particularly at that which is secret or forbidden, gains a sense of power by the act of looking and conversely is made to feel powerless by that which cannot be seen. The inquisitiveness of children is not just a means of finding out about the world; it is a way of constructing an identity within that world, an identity that is based upon a growing sense of a power relationship towards that world. The power to see is the power to understand, which leads to the power to possess and control, and Freud's theory of voyeurism is specifically associated with masculinity.

The look can produce different kinds of power: the power over others, as well as the power to create a desirable image of the self. The action of the shopper is pleasurable partly because we see in the windows of the stores reflections of an ideal self that is potentially achievable through the purchase of commodities. Freud talks of the narcissistic function of the look (its dwelling on one's pleasure in one's own image) as well as the voyeuristic (the pleasure of possessing another through the look). For window-shoppers the sense of possession that looking gives is clearly part of the appeal of the practice; for them, the shopping centre says, among other things, that all these goods are potentially yours, you possess the right to any of them. However, Freud would suggest that the looking which is such a crucial element in people's behaviour in the shopping centre is designed not to increase our understanding of others, but to increase our understanding of ourselves. What we admire in the windows is our own reflection, just as Narcissus did when he looked into the pool of water.

In his *Ecrits*, Lacan took Freud's theories a little further by

Reflections. Tricks with mirrors are common at shopping centres. Like the eighteenth-century architectural use of mirrors they double space and double a crowd, but these mirror surfaces are not flat and rational; they break up the image and disperse it over a bewildering set of vistas, creating multiple selves that are distorted, fragmented, glittering and unreal. They work on notions of plenitude, of looking and being looked at, and shatter the boundaries between the imagined and the real. A reflecting escalator like this has the attraction and the terror of magic, because the images are too fluid and out of control— unlike the commodities behind the shop windows, ideal images which appear more real, more controllable, and less threatening, by contrast.

suggesting that all children go through an important stage of de-velopment called 'the mirror phase'. In this children are fascinated by their reflection because this phase occurs when their bodies are inefficient and inadequate—they simply do not do what the child 'knows' they ought to. In the mirror the child sees its ideal, imag-inary self freed from the inadequacies of the real body. In this gap, this difference between the imaginary and the real, desire is born. According to Lacan this is the origin of one of our main motiva-tions throughout our lives: the motivation to seek pleasure. Conse-quently, pleasure is produced to the extent that an activity satisfies desire by closing the gap between the imaginary and the real. This is particularly applicable to our construction of identity by shopping. What these affordable, accessible commodities are saying is that you *can* narrow this gap; the gulf between the real you and the imaginary you is bridgeable; look, you can see it is, here is your imaginary self reflected back at you from the 'mirror-windows'.

The pleasure of being looked at is thus prised loose from the possessive power of the male voyeur. A woman can find a feminine pleasure in dress and accessories that is part of her power to construct her own public identity independent of the male gaze. Indeed, some fashions seem to take features that mark women's status as fetish objects for men and recycle them as challenges to, or even denials of, the male gaze. Signs of bondage, leather, skimpy clothes and aggressively bared skin can be read as women incorporating signs of patriarchy into a feminine system of meanings, a feminine pleasure in, and control over, her own image.

The 'production of pleasure', though, is not only explicable through psychoanalytic theory. In our earlier analyses of the activities of youth culture on the beach, in the pub and in the video parlours, we stressed the important role the body plays in both pleasure and individuality. The body is the source of the strongest sense of our own identity and difference. However much of our consciousness, our taste or our attitudes may have been formed by social conditions, our body appears to be uniquely ours, given us by 'nature' not 'culture'. Of course, being the complicated mixture of forces that we are, we can never allow the body to remain with such a singular, simple meaning for us. So we immediately allow social pressures to work on it and try to change it to what society wants at any one time. We might do this by dieting or exercise, by shaping and colouring its extremities—particularly hair and nails—and by painting designs on it that emphasise some features at the expense of others. This is equally true of more primitive societies than ours, emphasising the lack of distance between cultures when it comes to the more basic features of social organisation.

When we shop in order to construct an identity through an image, the body is our necessary starting point; it is our original source of a sense of identity, and the clothes and accessories that we buy function to enhance its individuality at the same time as they connect it to a particular social group. So it is little surprise to find that these shopping centres are celebrations of the body and its senses. It is through the operation of the senses that we become most aware of our bodies. Centrepoint uses words like 'exciting', 'enchanting', 'magical' or 'dazzling' to describe the atmosphere, predicting a physical, sensual response to it. Carillon's advertisements describe it in this way:

> From early morning to well after sunset, Carillon graces its patron's senses with the sounds of water, music, colour, and myriad delicious aromas which waft constantly about the fascinating collection of balconies, staircases and malls.

Most centres are well equipped with places to eat and drink, and with hairdressers and beauty consultants, and go out of their way to provide a rich and constantly changing diet of sensual stimulation.

In such suburban shopping centres as Sydney's Roselands, or Brisbane's Indooroopilly Shoppingtown the stage area offers other kinds of spectacle and stimulation as it serves to bring the worlds of entertainment and shopping closer together; it is used for fashion parades, demonstrations, live television shows, visits from personalities, children's entertainments in school holidays or community theatrical or musical performances. Fashion parades, in particular, conflate shopping and theatre by animating shop windows, and putting them on stage, as display becomes performance. Window-shoppers become an audience of spectators, the 'patron's senses' oversupplied as the glamour of show-biz is added to the glitter of shopping. The conflation of shopping, leisure and entertainment takes shopping out of the realm of domestic chores and attempts to rescue it from the mundane, to relocate it in the 'freedom' of leisure and entertainment.

As shoppers select their commodities/identities, the role played by individual taste within an exciting style is probably less comprehensively determined than most of our other social and cultural choices. Whatever the actual selections made, it is the opportunity given to the individual to use her imagination to create something new, something that will be uniquely hers, that confirms shopping as a leisure activity which is significantly opposed to work. The creative use of shopping by suburban housewives, as well as the popularity of shopping as a lunchtime activity among city workers, makes this structural opposition clear. Shopping whether it be actual purchasing or window-shopping is situated at the crucial interface between individual desire and social control; its special feature is that it gives precedence to individual desire. Work, on the other hand, while also operating at this interface, accords its precedence firmly to social control.

The Appeal of the New

One of the most important qualities of the city and suburban shopping centres such as Centrepoint or Roselands is newness, originality. Centrepoint presents itself in its publicity as the location of fashion, the trends, the new. Newness implies originality and creativity, and this is important from both the producers' and consumers' points of view. The fashion industry has frequently been criticised for creating artificial newness and therefore artificial obsolescence in order to boost its profits. Fashions change in order to make women buy the new long before the old has worn out. While this is true as far as it goes, it does not go far enough because it fails to address the question of why the consumer *wants* to be up to date. In failing to address this question, such accounts imply the answer is obvious: consumers are dupes that the industry can manipulate into any behaviour that suits it. These commonsense explanations are inadequate, and to find out why we must explore some alternatives.

The desire to be up to date, and there is plenty of evidence that this is a common desire, cannot be entirely created by slick publicity. Advertising works best when it links a product to already established desires. Lacan's theory about the origin of desire in the gap between the real and the imaginary is a suggestive one, but we need to stress that the imaginary is not a product of nature, something born into us, but a product of culture, something that we are born into. Western societies have a powerful ideology of progress that sees history and the passage of time as a natural process of change. Of course this is not natural but cultural—other societies see time and history as circular, repetitive. For such societies, change and the new are not markers of progress and the passage of time, but of disruption. For us, however, the desire to be up to date and trendy fits particularly well with the ideology of progress. This ideology is particularly potent (by which we mean it fits well with, and explains, the conditions of social existence) for two specific groups: one is Australians, and the other is youth.

One of the ways in which modern Australia, as a young and colonialised country, has consciously defined itself is through images of development, of leaving the past behind. This is noticeable in the 1980s as we continue to shake off the bonds with Britain in order to define a national identity that is distinctive and to construct an identification with a modernity that is within reach rather than an ancient European history which is not. Newness, for the nineteenth century and for early Australia, was not a valuable commodity. As Australia has become more confident in its assertion of the value of its specific qualities, newness and Australianness have come to fit together well. These shopping centres are constructions of newness—their bright glittering lights make the commodities sparkle as though they were minted yesterday; the shiny ceilings, walls and floors possess the cleanliness of high technology; acres of plate glass with never a smear or finger mark all add up to an overwhelming impression of brand newness. No hint of the shabby, the worn, is allowed to creep in.

In the ideology of progress the new is king, and in its most culturally specific formulations the new is also necessarily Australian.

The new is also youth, and these shopping centres are filled with the young. Centrepoint's demographics point to the majority of its customers occupying the 15–25 age group. The ideology of progress works well for the confident young (that is, those who have jobs, education and money—not so many these days) who are the ones attracted by such centres. For youth sees the new as a necessary part of the process of maturing; leaving the old behind is leaving the younger immature self behind, too. So the young are determinedly trendy, up to date, and these shopping centres are, as Centrepoint puts it, 'trend-packed'.

There is strong ideological resistance to this, of course, so that the commitment to the new or the fashionable is subject to a great deal of negativity. The commonsense egalitarian ethic which crops up elsewhere in our readings is often mobilised to produce a suspicion and fear of difference, limiting that trendiness to variations of an accepted style rather than something disruptively original. A version of fashion is often the butt of the attacks made from a commonsense jokey perspective, as the photos and comments from *The Australian*'s 'Australian Woman' page indicate. In these two examples, fashion is represented as inherently silly, unAustralian and, implicitly, something most Australian women can be expected to reject. The comfortable sense of a commonality with the readership enables the caption writer to make relatively gratuitous jokes safely, secure in the self-evident ridiculousness of this kind of clothing (fruit on one's shoes, really!) while attempting to get credit for an irreverence and subversive humour that rightly belongs to Linda de Beer and Vera. The similarity between the look modelled by Vera

All is forgiven, Carmen Miranda

─Lowdown from Paris─

SOME might say the young fashion parade in West Berlin yesterday was enough to send you up the wall. This knitted ensemble is called Strange Fruit and is a creation of **Linda de Beer**, who is from Amsterdam. The model, whose name is **Vera**, is wearing fruit on her shoes — a bit of lemon on the sole perhaps — and is carrying yet more in the string bag which she is about to catapult through the air, possibly aiming it at the designer — AP picture

From the 'Australian Woman' page in the Australian newspaper, 16 October 1985

Yes, but how low can you go? A model presents an ensemble of the spring-summer collection by French designer Jean Colonna in Paris. It is a Spanish type of puckered chest front on a bust-knotted brassiere kind of shirt over a low belted miniskirt-like piece of fabric, topped by a long colourful assorted fabric overall. The model wears this attractive summer ensemble with a pair of large dark glasses because she doesn't want anyone to recognise her.

and that modelled by female pop stars such as Madonna underlines what is less apparent in *The Australian*: that this is a look identified with youth but which no sensible mature woman would wear. There are clear limits, then, to the degree of individuality allowed the shopper and the wearer, set by asking them to justify their image against standards other than those of originality or difference. It is not surprising that the greatest adventure for the fashionable young occurs in a form where experiment and difference have been allowed and contained: the T-shirt, an object in which the class aspect of fashion is buried.

The T-shirt is ubiquitous in shops these days, as it suits our ideology as perfectly as it suits our climate. It is mass produced, cheap and available to all, yet it is individualised so that we rarely see two people wearing identical designs. It expresses conformity as well as individual difference, community at the same time as identity. It is informal, but can be dressed up by arty designs to suit formal occasions. It is also disposable, and can be cheaply and easily updated. The choice of a new T-shirt encapsulates much of what we have been describing, the choice of the new, the individual, the fashionable, the Australian, and the personal possession. What it tends to deny, though, even if unconsciously, is the subject of the next section, the role of class.

Shopping for Class

A necessary product of newness is variety, for there must be something new for each individual. These shopping centres provide a fantastic variety of commodities, yet this variety exists within an overall homogeneity of style. This difference within similarity becomes a metaphor for the relationship of the individual with the social. The similarity of style is that which connects us with others; being a common factor it becomes a marker of group membership—a sort of tribal dress or decoration. The variety is used to make individual differences within the style, to identify the individual within the group. The difference between style and taste is never easy to define, but style tends to be more centred on the group or the social whereas taste is more concerned with the individual. Both, however, are traversed by markers of class. Style tells us about the broad generic patterns of class, money and age, while taste tells us about the particular mode of insertion of the individual into these social patterns. Class and money differences are understated in shopping centres, for fairly obvious reasons: there is little point in excluding buyers from the market place. However, the design of shops and their use of space, as well as their location within the shopping complex, provide evidence that such class differences do exist and are of commercial importance.

The key opposition here is that between democracy or 'cheapness', on the one hand, and exclusiveness or 'money is no object', on the other. Centrepoint provides a clear example of this opposition at work.

Those shops with low-priced goods that appeal to everyone, such as newsagents, card shops or chemists, are the most 'democratic' shops. They tend not to have windows, but open fronts; the boundaries between their territory and the public concourse are deliberately leaky, so their goods spill over into the pedestrian

'*Come on in, I'm a specialty shop,* specially for you. If I suit your taste, I'll have the identity you're looking for. I'm available to all; plenty here for everyone. But I have a territory, an identity, a specialty. I only hope it matches yours.'

The windows are peep holes showing that the goods in them are multiplied a hundred times in the shop. And the images bought are multiplied and sent back from the reflections outside.

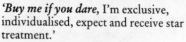

'*Buy me if you dare,* I'm exclusive, individualised, expect and receive star treatment.'

Shop window and lighting emphasise the differences between the buyer and the rest of society and the boundaries between the shop and the public. No mass availability of this unique piece.

'*Egalitarian, mate,* no exclusive territory for me, no boundary between me and you.' So, of course, it sells T-shirts.

areas. The distinction between the public-democratic and the private-exclusive is minimised. In the 'middle-class' range, that of the medium-priced trendy fashion shops selling clothes, bags, shoes and accessories, the boundaries tend to be marked a little more clearly but not exclusively. They will have windows, but racks of shoes or shirts will often push out on to the concourse. And the windows will tend to be crammed full of goods, tastefully arranged according to colour and style but still giving the impression of plenitude, of availability to all. There is plenty for everyone, they seem to say, all you need is the tastes we cater for. These windows, too, reveal the shop; the multitude of goods within them never obscures the even greater number of goods within the shop itself. The lighting of both the shop and the window is bright, and designed to give an identity to the shop that differentiates it from the concourse and from others. As different individuals construct their images within the similarity of fashion, so different shops construct their identity. Even the more democratic shops, such as the food bars on the bottom level of Centrepoint or the MLC arcade, which are identical in their exterior features, will differ from each other in their signs, their interior colour schemes, staff uniforms and lighting. The windows and lighting of these middle-range shops create an identity for them that differentiates them from each other and from the public areas, but still opens them up and invites the browser inside.

While the 'democratic' shops tend not to stress their own identity, and the 'middle-class' shops identify themselves as different but still available, the 'upper-class' shops—such as those in the Gallery level in Centrepoint—are exclusive. Their windows have fewer goods in them, signalling the opposite of mass availability; their lighting is more subdued, with highlights on the individual commodity; and the shop behind the window is much less easily seen. Sometimes, indeed, its secretion is such that the explicit intention seems to be one of exclusion. The contrast in lighting styles between middle- and upper-class windows is a contrast in class taste and social presence. The highlights on the exclusive commodity, a fur coat or an haute couture dress, suggests that the wearer will be in the spotlight, picked out from the others. The overall bright lighting in the middle-class windows suggested that the wearers will be members of the group that shares their style and taste. In theatrical terms, it is the difference between lighting the star and lighting the chorus line. The windows of these more upmarket shops exclude the mass viewer and signal the limited availability of their commodities and thus of the identities they offer. The exclusiveness is clear in Centrepoint's drawing of a comparison between its Gallery level and London's Bond Street or New York's Fifth Avenue.

In Centrepoint, and in many other shopping centres we have visited, there is a deliberate policy to class these three types of shop by the physical level, each of the three levels corresponding to a class style. It is interesting to note that our culture's metaphoric conceptualisation of classes as though they existed in vertical spatial relationship to each other is treated here as though it were literal, not metaphoric; the upper-class shops 'naturally' on the highest floor, the democratic ones 'naturally' on the lowest. Of course, there is a practical marketing reason in Centrepoint, and for most others whose entry floor is the ground floor: most of the through-traffic occurs on the Pitt St level, and so the appeal of those shops needs to be aimed at the widest possible market. In a suburban centre such as Roselands, despite the relative lack of explicitly upper-class shops, the class relations within the range of democratic and middle-class shops are structured in the same way, as if the spatial metaphor we commonly use to express moral and social values has been made concrete.

The practice is not universal and does seem to be implicated in the class structure and ideology of the community it serves. In Brisbane, for instance, possibly the most working class and demographically heterogeneous of our capital cities (it lacks Sydney's Eastern Suburbs or North Shore, but possesses pockets of upper-class dwellings cheek by jowl with working-class housing), the vertical arrangement is less obvious. The spread at Indoorpilly Shoppingtown is horizontal, and shops are less clearly divided in hierarchical, class terms. There is no 'gallery' level here, and the general range of discourses of fashion and style is narrow. This is true of the city centre in Brisbane also, and it possesses fewer Centrepoint-style arcades than other cities of comparable size. Expansion is under way in this area at the time of writing, and it will be interesting to see if the dominant Australian construction or the local Brisbane inflections will prevail in such projected complexes as the Riverside development.

Shifting Centres

Shopping may seem to be a modern pastime, connected with materialism and consumerism but with little else. Yet, the market place has always been a central structural feature—economic, physical and social—of communities. Part of the yearning for the integrated village community of Europe that surfaced most explicitly in Don Dunstan's television documentaries but which is present in critiques of Australian culture since at least the 1920s recognises how clearly the market place serves its function in such social structures. The European market place, often unchanged in its physical features for centuries, is admittedly a more romantic place than the concrete boxes surrounded by car parks which serve the same function in Australian suburbs. The sidewalk-styled cafes which proliferate in such shopping centres, and the European and exotic foods sold in such cafes, indicate that there is a deliberate attempt to reconnect our version of the market place with the European. Centrepoint explicitly invokes Paris in its upper level, and Carillon goes to the most clear extreme in its mimicking of European village structures in its layout and design. The choice of a carillon as a centrepiece is itself in deference to European models. Not all such processes result in imitation, however. The Australian coffee lounge is a unique object composed of the two discourses of the Australian and the European but different from either. Its success as a cultural form has sent many Australian tourists in England, particularly, to the brink of despair in the attempt to find its counterpart there.

As this example indicates, while our suburban centres may not come up to the European standards of people like Don Dunstan, that should not blind us to the fact that they do serve similar functions but with Australian inflections. They do this by providing us with culturally specific transformations of the European (and American) forms, transformations that have a distinctive Australian history.

The history of shopping in Australia starts out with the country store and with the combination of department stores and corner shops that had evolved by the mid-1920s in most of our cities. To deal with the city alone, the division between the services provided in the city and those in the suburbs—the department store and the corner shop—is a division between different definitions of the community. The city, for example, was not a place in which one lived, but it operated as a giant market place for the more exciting and individualised. The city had its own logic of development, while the suburb evolved in what seemed to be a more organic, community-based, way. The development of the suburban shopping centre was one of accretion: the corner store was joined by other, slightly more specialised stores—the greengrocer and the butcher, for instance—and its user was the housewife buying her everyday needs. Many of the functions now served by supermarkets or by advances in technology such as the refrigerator were once served by delivery men—the baker, the iceman, the rabbitoh, the greengrocer's cart, and so on. Such services ameliorated the labour of the housewife and were an extension of the domestic realm. The myth we have of the personal nature of one's dealings with the local shop proprietor is one that asserts the close connection between the merchants and the community in the suburbs, as well as embodying a different view of the way in which the housewife should and did spend her day. The time-consuming process of shopping daily and in a large number of different shops constructs a different version of women's labour and their family role, as well as a different version of the service provided by retail trade.

The city department store, and after the 1930s depression such chain-stores as G.J. Coles', did not have this domestic, service role, but provided access to the wider dimensions of consumption. The success of the city department store, offering the full range of services under the one roof, helped to place the city as an important but different part of the shopping structure. However, it also probably helped to lay the ground for the most important intervention in the nature of shopping in Australia, the growth of the suburban supermarket, and its logical progression, the shopping centre or shopping town as we now know it.

The supermarket arrived in the early 1960s, and originally it provided the bulk and banal materials of life—a centralised and magnified corner shop. Unlike the city department store but like the city chain-store, the supermarket in its earliest formations was geared much more to actual shopping than to window-shopping. In the early 1960s the visit to the city was still an adventure; after the first few times, a visit to the supermarket was not. Whereas many shoppers left the city centre, as they do now, with full imaginations and memories of pleasure but with few actual commodities, shoppers rarely left the supermarket empty handed. The spread of car ownership from the 1950s onwards assisted the growth of supermarkets and their large car parks. They were the original 'one-stop shop', and they grew as a direct consequence of four factors: home deliveries of foodstuffs were never fully re-established after the war; car ownership approached one per family, and soon many families had two; the ownership of refrigerators necessary to store the bulk purchases increased; and, finally, the major means of mass advertising for mass-produced food, television, arrived.

Advances in technology do not in themselves produce changes in cultural behaviour and meanings. They have to coincide with the myths of the culture for this sort of change to occur. These technological changes fitted the dominant mythology of the 1960s perfectly and, in most cases, still do. As we shall see when we look at the Sydney Opera House, the postwar period is one of reconstruction, not simply as a result of social distortions and dislocations produced by the war, but in order to reconstruct a more confident image of Australia. One of the important elements in this new vision of Australia is a casting off of some of the ties to an older and discredited Europe and the embracing of the signifiers of modernity, of the new, from an heroic America. The suburban home is partly derived from this movement. One of the first of the supermarket chains to make an impact here provides a good example of this process. G.J. Coles' stores started out as cheap chain-stores, expanding dramatically during the depression years. For its intervention in the supermarket sector, it became Coles New World, drawing its name from the establishment of America and its appropriation of American models to create a 'new world' for the shopper. Its newness was stressed with the sign of the rocket soaring over the new world, drawing on myths of modernity, of the future, of the connection between technological innovation and the Russian–American space race which was, within the decade, to land a man on the moon. The car, the refrigerator, the rocket to the moon, were all signs of the times, and signs that the supermarket either supported or appropriated so that it, too, became a sign of those times.

This did not last. The metropolitan centre still meant the adventurous, the fashionable, and the up-to-date. While the supermarket presented a new way of shopping, it was a new way of shopping for the mundane and the basic. The supermarket was functional rather than magical, and the shopper would use it differently to the city centre; the shopper in the supermarket was the housewife, defined by her social role, whereas in the city she could still be the individual searching for a more precise identity.

As the supermarket 'bred', through its attracting of speciality shops into its ambit, so the shopping town concept—the large self-contained block of shops surrounded by parking space and offering commodities for the most exotic as well as the most functional of needs—developed. The early examples, Roselands or Chadstone, were placed in outer suburbs from which the visit to the city had become increasingly difficult. These centres had many of the features offered by the city: department stores moved into direct competition with the suburban shops and became intrinsic features; the speciality stores were in many cases simply expansions of existing city chains, and the supermarket operated to provide the need for regular weekly visits. The city, with its interest in the new, its satisfaction of the individual as well as the functional, had invaded the suburbs.

By the end of the 1960s the impact of the new suburban shopping centres, with their mixture of the community shopping place and the magical city, was sufficient to worry city retailers. Large parts of Sydney, by the early 1970s, were seen to be dying. The Haymarket end of town, once dominated by two large department stores, Anthony Hordern's and Marcus Clarke's became seedy and unfrequented by shoppers. Marcus Clarke's closed, and its department store function went with it; Hordern's became a minor department store and was saved only by its moving into the centres in suburbs such as Chatswood. This was the context in which Centrepoint opened in 1972, as the inner heart of Sydney was fighting back against the growth of the suburban shopping centres in order to re-establish itself as the centre of activity and excitement through such developments as the closing of Martin Place to traffic in order to recover it 'for the people'. Not only was this an attempt to inscribe the city back into the community, but an attempt to regain the leadership in determining the new, the fashionable and the up-to-date.

As Centrepoint's own publicity points out, 'it set new shopping standards which over the next twelve years were to be copied by many developers and retail traders throughout Australia' (*Shopping Centre News* November/December, 1984). The success of this imitation both within the city and within the suburban shopping centres can be gauged by the need Centrepoint expressed in 1984 to refurbish and to recover its position as the 'most exciting shopping experience in Sydney'. The Sydney Tower is another shot in the battle to demonstrate the pre-eminence of city excitement over suburban convenience. Similar urban redevelopment in other cities—the Queen St. Mall in Brisbane, for instance—can be seen as responses to the same threat: the death of the city and the fragmentation of the urban unit into the smaller suburban communities and their focal shopping places.

Despite such strategies, the suburban centre, with its meanings of value, cheapness and plenty for all, still forms the economic base of the shopping system. The downtown centre, built around the speciality stores selling social identities, is the superstructure. That they compete for dominance is due to the fact that they are both part of the same mythology. The downtown centre is what it is because the suburban centre now exists in the same system, and we shop in the way we do downtown because, on other days of the week, we shop differently in the suburbs. But there are similarities between the two types of centre, as well as differences. The suburban one has, around its central department stores and supermarkets, roughly the same shops as are found in the city. They also have similar facilities for seeing and being seen, for the spectacle of shopping. For some of the users of the suburban centre, too, they function in many of the same ways as the city version.

Teenagers, particularly young ones, use these centres as free meeting places. Particularly on late shopping night, large numbers of them will meet to stroll up and down the concourses; to window-shop, to display the clothes that give them both an identity and a membership in a particular subculture that their everyday school clothes deny, and generally to see and be seen. For them, these centres are not primarily functional places for buying but are, like the downtown centres, places where new identities and social relationships can be constructed (albeit from a more narrow range of alternatives)—places that can be made into their territory as opposed to the school and the home which are controlled by others.

The ways in which both kinds of centre enter the world of entertainment has already been mentioned. For the city centre this merely reinforces the idea of the city as the hub; in the suburban centre it mediates the isolation of the suburb from this hub, and as an amelioration of the role of the housewife it is an important mode of access to the wider world. Where the working woman under the age of 30 is the dominant group of user of the city centre, the housewife is the dominant group in the suburbs, and it is her usage that is the most important in determining its function.

The function of the suburban shopping centre is difficult to read from its exterior, from its structure, as we have done with other texts, because it is extremely contradictory. Contradictions can be seen in features of the design. The exteriors of these huge structures have large areas of brick and concrete, walls unrelieved by windows, and usually small and surprisingly inconspicuous entrances—almost like a castle standing in a moat of car parks. They give the impression from the outside of being self-contained strongrooms (or warehouses in a lower-classs inflection) of treasure, which have no need to attract or call the passerby inside. People come with the intention of entering; they do not wander casually in as they do downtown. Inside, the exits are equally unmarked—the commercial motivation for this is deliberate, to encourage people to pass more shops and thus have more temptations to buy as they look for an exit. But the effect is more than behavioural, for it also supports the impression that they are self-sufficient worlds, significantly opposed to and palliatives for the outside world of home and work. This opposition works on a number of axes: unlike the corner store, the shopping centre strives to be social and public, not private or domestic; like the city, it strives to be part of leisure, entertainment, an occasion in the week—not work, the humdrum, the mundane; for the individual, it works to give a sense of plenitude, of richness, as opposed to the economic restrictions of everyday life.

Such oppositions are also those we could find if we returned to our mythical European market place, romanticised by the tourist but used by its communities in similar ways to those outlined above. While the shopping centre is perhaps not as decorative or as quaint as the market place in Perugia which Don Dunstan filmed for his ABC documentaries, the lack of photogenic qualities is not mirrored by an empty social function. In fact, if we were to examine the history of the decline of the corner shop and the change in the rituals of shopping over this century in Australia, we might conclude that the reason these centres have taken over from the corner shops has at least as much to do with the way they have met imaginative needs that are those of the community, but that are unsatisfied in the experience of work and home, as it has to do with their convenience and cheapness.

6 Tourism

The short trip

In 1982–83 Australians spent 221 500 000 nights in beds other than their own. And those were only the ones recorded by the Tourism Commission. Each of those away-nights had to be at least 40 km from home, but not overseas, to qualify. The great majority of these trips were for pleasure or holiday. Put another way, the statistics tell us that in one year Australians made over 23 million trips of more than 40 km involving at least one night's stop.

Of course, the statistics tell us only what we already know, that Australians are restless, always on the move. It's tempting to look back at our 'recent' immigration to explain this—seeing Australians as people without deep community roots who came here to find something better over the horizon and whose perspective has never shortened in its focus. Australians are simply not stay-at-homes in origin or outlook. But, like most appeals to origins, these explanations cannot tell us the whole story. All this activity happens now, and its complex reasons and meanings exist in the everyday present.

The most obvious point about a holiday trip is that it moves the family away from home and away from work. It interrupts the normal, secular life and transfers it into the abnormal or the 'sacred', the 'magic'. The word holiday was originally 'holy day', a day in which neither wage-labour nor domestic-labour was allowed its usual dominance over the thinking, behaviour and therefore social identities of the people. Holidays are breaks from the normal construction of social identity by work and home. But besides finding their meaning in what they reject, or leave behind, holidays must also be understood in terms of what they promise. A trip is both a trip away and a trip towards.

Let us take a family camping trip as an example. It involves the family, but it also involves a redefinition of roles within the family, in particular the roles of mother and father. Western societies typically associate the indoors with women and the outdoors with men, but in Australia the opposition seems particularly strongly marked. The civilising force of the home is a feminine force, and Chapter 2 has shown how the kitchen, the centre of feminine control, has become increasingly central in the suburban house. The extension of domesticity to the outdoor living area can be seen as a further piece of feminine colonisation, pushing the men, their barbecues and beer further to the fringes of the garden.

Australian ideology teaches males an extreme definition of masculinity in which notions of power and control, self-reliance and independence, and separation from the feminine are absolutely central, but these are not just the qualities from which this ideology constructs its notion of masculinity; they are also the characteristics upon which it claims Australia was built. The construction of Australia and the construct of masculinity are almost inseparable. But these 'natural', central values are under threat in many aspects of Australian life. If the suburban house is one example, the workplace is another. As Australia follows the rest of Western societies into corporate and international capitalism, so the corporations and firms in which so many of us work become larger, more impersonal, more bureaucratised. Government agencies consistently increase their regulation of social life, and the proposal to introduce the Australia Card is seen by its opponents as the culmination of this tendency. The independence and self-reliance that 'made Australia what it is', and made the Australian male what he likes to think he is, is under threat from all directions.

In the pub (see Chapter 1) the male can shake himself free of these contradictions and be a 'man' amongst 'men'. But the pub always, for the married man, carries a tinge of guilt centred on the wife and family left at home and the avoidance of responsibility. In contrast, on a camping trip the male can attempt to rediscover his 'true' masculinity without the guilt, for he takes his family with him. The open air is the male domain, nature is male: indoors, civilisation, culture are female and are left behind, in imagination at least. The male is typically in charge of loading the car and of driving it, and while the mother may be unable to shake off entirely her role in organising and preparing food, her husband will typically do far more over the camp fire, barbecue or camping gas stove than he ever would in the kitchen at home.

The move back to a less threatened masculinity in nature involves, perhaps contradictorily, a weakening of gender roles and
the gender identities that go with them. Husband and wife share
tasks that would, at home, tend to be specific to one of them and in
so doing experience both a sense of release from conventions and an
interrogation of these conventions and the social values that produce them. Camping is not just an escape from the suburbs but
a way of exploring and experiencing different and 'freer' social
relations.

But paradoxically campers allow themselves to be organised in
campsites in a way that diminishes the threat of the camp to the
ideology of the suburb. For while the *idea* of camping may be a
return to our roots in nature and an escape from the artificiality of
the suburbs, the experience of camping has involved a progressive
commodification of the simple life into something approaching the
capitalisation of the suburban home. Most suburbs have at least one
specialist camping shop that is packed with tents, furniture and
equipment. The comforts of home and the suburbs that cannot be
easily transported are also provided at many sites—the deli, laundry, showers, pool, games room. The presence of the conveniences
that actually make the suburb such a practical and popular place to
live means that the positive aspects of the suburban home are not
under the same sort of interrogation as its more constricting ones.
For while the campsite may look like a suburb in miniature with
the tents and caravans neatly arrangd, it does differ considerably.

The most liberating difference of all is its temporary nature. In
the campsite, the Australian camping family may not have moved
that much closer to nature, but it has freed itself from the permanence of the home. For the home is deeply contradictory. Every
settler's dream was a house and land, and Australia has become a
property-owning democracy: its proportion of public housing is
far lower than most other industrial societies. The house has become a metaphor for the self, its bricks and mortar an extension of
the body. The builders and real estate agents stress the uniqueness
and character of their houses, trying to disguise their underlying
similarities with superficial individualisations. Like the people they
shelter, the suburban houses form a community of taste within
which features and commodities work to construct an individuality
that is not disruptive to the community.

The house may have become a metaphor for the self and the
body, but unlike the body it is fixed and immovable. It anchors the
Australian to the suburb, denying the freedom of the bush and the

open plains. While allowing the owners the sense of freedom to be themselves, it is also a prison, particularly for the independence and freedom that are so central to the notion of masculinity. The camp-sites and the camping shops offer all the comforts and security of the suburb, without demanding that they are paid for by a loss of freedom: the campsite offers mobility as opposed to anchorage.

The Australian writer, Meaghan Morris, has suggested that the Australian obsession with the motor car is not just a reflection of that felt elsewhere in the Western world but is a positive expression of our self-image as a developing society. The physical mobility of the car is a metaphor for progress as well as a masculine expression of freedom and power. Like the campsite, the car bears meanings of both the material benefits of progress and the freedom and mobility of the older, pioneering Australia that is so important to our imagination but so difficult to keep alive in our contemporary social conditions.

This desire for mobility and the freedom associated with it is deeply embedded in Western popular culture and shows itself in such common generic characteristics as the Western hero riding off into the sunset or the popularity of road movies and novels. But Australia inflects and intensifies this desire: the Mad Max movies, despite their international appeal, are quintessentially Australian. The vastness of the continent, its huge distances within itself and from the rest of the Western world, produce a sense that no Aus-tralian is complete until he or she has experienced them. 'We've crossed the Nullarbor' is a bumper sticker that reflects a parti-cularly Australian pride and a particularly Australian necessity. For travelling the wide open spaces is a comfortable reenactment of the pioneer experience, and part of its pleasure is a conscious, and often spoken, sense of the difference between modern travel and the early settlers who conquered these distances without the aid of bitumen and the internal combustion engine. Travel connects us with our history in addition to giving us a metaphor for the future.

Travel, identity and the look

The desire to travel is not, of course, unique to Australians, though Australians do appear to experience it particularly strongly. It is common to the industrialised world, and rising levels of affluence are almost invariably reflected in increased tourism. The number of travel agents is a fair indicator of the comparative affluence of a society.

The reasons for this are complex and well hidden. Television and the rest of the media show us the rest of the world daily and familiarise us with it. Western industrialism has internationalised itself, and a country's economy is increasingly explained in terms of the international economy. The nation, the region, the neighbourhood seem increasingly inadequate as sites of social understanding or of social identity. We are constantly being shown what is happening over the horizon, constantly being offered national and international news and images. Our television and cinema fiction is frequently set in American cities or exotic locations, and no TV quiz game is complete without a trip as one of the main prizes. All this serves to give our suburban neighbourhood, however comfortable and happily inhabited, a sense of the prison: its limitations are constantly on view.

But the media do not merely give us the global village, telling us that the rest of the world is our backyard; they construct for us a position of power in that village. Their Western-centred discourses, their white-eyed cameras, construct the rest of the world as there for *us*. The capitalist political and economic attempt to colonise the world may have failed and may now be viewed with increasing suspicion by some of those, at least, whose compatriots and forebears were the most enthusiastic colonisers. But the colonisation by looking, possession by the gaze, is continuing unabated, and tourism is merely an individualised extension of the symbolic colonisation by the media. 'I am monarch of all I survey' expresses more than Robinson Crusoe's satisfaction with his island life: it results from the intimate relationship of human beings with 'their' land, the pride of possession felt by every landowner from the English aristocrat, through the early Australian settler to the proud possessor of a mortgage on a quarter-acre suburban block. The international tourist may well be the contemporary colonist, but trips within Australia bear quite different meanings. Touring 'our country' is both a symbolic assertion of our 'ownership' of it and an affirmation of our identity as 'Australians' that such an ownership entails.

Looking is both enactment of possession and a construction of identity for the looker. Sydney Tower looks over the city; Brisbane is soon to build an even higher tower to give its citizens even greater power to visually possess their city than Sydneysiders have. Similarly, national parks have carefully constructed 'look-outs', or paths to carefully selected natural lookouts, from which we may not only wonder at the beauty and vastness of our land but also experience our identity in relation to it, reaffirm our rights to it, however historically insecure these rights may be.

The photograph is a symbolic enactment of this: each print or slide is a piece of our world that we are taking home with us. The camera may be the final agent of colonisation that constructs the rest of the world and its peoples as the picturesque to be captured and possessed by the photographer/tourist. But this is an inad-equate and uncharitable account of the pleasure that photographs provide for so many people. More positively, the tourist photo-graph inserts us into 'our' world. The photographer typically poses members of the family in the landscape, on the wonder of nature or looking over the view. The photograph relates the Australian and the landscape so that each gives meaning to the other. The family album is so much more than a collection of images of a visually colonised landscape; it is an imaginative statement of pleasure, pride, possession and identity.

Tourism is an essential part of late capitalist culture. It is an expression of a cultural dissatisfaction that the tourist industry has been quick to exploit. Australia has a particular inflection of this dissatisfaction and the ideology of which it is a part. Australian society is the most urbanised in the world, yet Australians believe, probably more strongly than any other Western nation, that they are 'naturally' rural people. Australian cities are recent, the Austra-lian sense of an independent national identity is young and still developing, and its differentness has long been mythologised in terms of landscape (nature) rather than of culture. So the cities, on the geographic but also symbolic fringe of the continent, have been neglected as a resource out of which to construct a social or a national identity. Only Sydney Harbour, with its bridge and its opera house and their magnificent natural setting, is rich enough in symbolism and history to provide an urban site powerful enough to produce a satisfying sense of identity. Apart from this, Australians must look elsewhere.

Ayers Rock is a convenient symbol for this search: it stands like the Holy Grail of the Australian tourist: it is everything that the white suburbs are not, yet remains accessible to those suburbs. Tourism constructs it by and for the white Australian, and in so doing, occasionally, for some, questions the adequacy of white history and white society to provide what the suburbs so patently fail to.

Ayers Rock and the tourist

Ayers Rock, the navel of Australia, the red centre, the heart—the common metaphors all attest that its centrality is not merely geographical. The power of the Rock's symbolism is as much a function of Australia's need for a national identity as it is of the identities that the Rock offers. In practice, of course, the way to understand the search is to look carefully at its object, and that is the way we intend to go.

Tourism involves a mixture of the strange and the familiar. The international hotels with their international cuisine and decor (albeit with local inflections) are set in unfamiliar and exotic locations. The strange is outside, ideally visible through the plate glass windows of the luxury suites, and accessible through tours, through guide books and souvenirs. The strange is there to be looked at and, essentially, photographed. Ayers Rock is described in the tourist literature as 'a photographer's paradise'. Another function the photograph does is to establish uniqueness within the familiar. Each photograph is unique, different from all others, yet instantly conventional, instantly recognisable. A tourist's photograph of Ayers Rock is a statement of uniqueness; it is of Ayers Rock and of nowhere else, it was at a particular moment in time, and it was taken by a particular individual. The three dimensions of uniqueness, place, time and the individual come powerfully together in the photograph, yet they work within the conventions of commonality: all photographs of Ayers Rock look similar, and in taking the photograph the tourist almost certainly has in mind the well-circulated images of what the rock 'really' does look like to the camera.

The camera is like the international hotel: it contains the contradictions of the unique strangeness of 'out there', with the conventional familiarity of 'in here'. Looking through the camera lens is like looking through the hotel's plate glass window: it is a way of standing inside culture observing nature. But within the difference there is similarity: the photograph, as we have seen, also inserts us in nature. Similarly, while the spectator-tourist may be separate from the view, he or she is also part of it: the view constructs and possesses the viewer just as much as it is constructed by him or her.

The advertising for the Sheraton Ayers Rock Hotel plays on and develops these themes. The Yulara resort is 'unique', the Rock is a 'special place', 'the world's greatest monolith', and it is there as a spectacle, a 'scene' with its 'incredible light shows at sunrise and sunset'. And, of course, it is to be seen from the familiar Sheraton Hotel which 'brings a modern luxury and international standards to this special place'. But this precariously resolved opposition between the uniquely strange and the conventionally familiar is set within others that work to establish what constitutes the strangeness of Ayers Rock and its difference from the mundane experience of the Australian or international tourist who visits it.

The Rock is a source of wonder in the world of the ordinary. The tourist is bombarded with facts and figures about it to enhance and justify the wonder that it naturally evokes. Thus the literature explains that it is 600 million years old, that the red desert surrounding it used to be a sea, that it is nearly 9 km round and is 348 m high, and, perhaps the greatest wonder of all, 'the Rock is so big that as it heats up or cools down it creates its own weather— including wind and clouds' and the accompanying photograph shows the unique rock-created cloud blowing off one end of it. But this source of wonderment with the power to create its own weather cannot be adequately explained by white science, for white science is part of the urban world that the tourist is seeking alternatives to.

All white science can do is provide a base for the 'true' wonderment of the Rock. This is expressed by words such as 'magic', 'mystique', 'mystery', "sacred', 'dreamtime', words with strong connotations of Aboriginality and of a timeless spiritual knowledge beyond that of mere science. In the Sheraton Hotel advertisement the phrase 'Where every spirit plays' works as richly and complexly as language in advertising typically does. 'Plays' opposes tourism and leisure to work, but also conveys a sense of freedom, of *free* play, as though the tourist will be liberated from the shackles of our mundane rational existence. 'Spirit' brings with it a sense of deep human universals that our rational, economically centred world has driven underground. The spirit of the individual tourist merges with the timeless spirit of the place, as though the experience frees the tourist from the constraints of the urban material world and inserts him or her into a mystical, spiritual, freer world in which white people's dreams can connect with the Aboriginal dreamtime.

This imaginary world, of course, does not exist. We construct it imaginatively as a response to our unspoken dissatisfaction with our everyday world and its narrow limits. We construct it, then, to provide alternatives to those elements of the everyday world that seem to comprise its limits: reason, materiality, tight time schedules, artificiality, its small scale, its ordinariness and its mere understandability.

And this is where the concept of Aboriginality is so important. We use the term 'Aboriginality' because it is clearly a term in a white discourse. It is a white concept that meets the needs of a white culture rather than one that provides an accurate understanding of Aboriginal peoples. The role played by Aboriginality in white people's understanding of Australia and their own position in the nation is fraught with political, historical and psychological problems; so much insecurity and guilt pervades the subject that it would need a far longer and more incisive book than this one to attempt to do it justice. But Aboriginality is such a central element in the meanings of Ayers Rock and the red centre that we have to attempt it.

The main point to make is that Australian meanings of Aboriginality are multiple and circulate in a number of different cultural domains. Thus the various domains of history, of politics, of law and order, of economics (especially mining and property ownership), of education, of social welfare, of sport, of the arts, of tourism, and so on, each have a set of meanings of Aboriginality. As each of these domains is relatively autonomous from all of the others, the meanings of Aboriginality that circulate in the Australian culture at large are varied, contradictory, and extremely difficult to pin down. The domain of art, for example, in which Aboriginal art is now highly valued (both financially and aesthetically) circulates a completely different set of meanings from those current in, say, the domain of law and order where Aborigines are seen as potential and probable criminals. It is the domain of tourism that we are primarily interested in here and the set of meanings that are typical to it. But its autonomy is only relative. It obviously overlaps with that of art, for example, and some of the literature prepared for tourists links it to the economic—it explains how Aboriginal peoples have a completely different relationship with the land to that of whites, and that the white notion of owning land is irreconcilable with the Aborigine's sense of belonging to the land.

The meanings given to Aboriginality by tourism are obviously meanings for white people. They can vary from ones exploiting the difference between white and black (Aboriginals are made into objects of wonder, much like Ayers Rock) to ones that attempt to go some way to narrowing the gap between the two cultures. There is some hope that some of the understanding gained by urban whites touring the red centre may, eventually, leak out of the domain of tourism and into that of politics. But only some.

Thus when in 1985 the Rock was 'given back' to Aboriginal 'ownership' or 'control' (note the white terms of economic exchange and ownership) the press reported fears about the move, fears particularly that Aboriginal control would threaten white access to, or use of, the Rock. These fears derived from meanings of Aboriginality current in the political and economic domains; they constructed Aboriginality as a political and economic threat to white control of the nation and its land. In the domain of tourism, however, the return to Aboriginal control would appear to add to the Rock's desired meanings for whites: its sacredness and Aboriginality are an important reason for whites to go there.

Part of the power of the Azaria Chamberlain story derives from its location at the Rock. There is a sense of a non-human spirit at the centre of Australia that is both dangerous but also spiritually refreshing to white people. The novel (and subsequent film) *Picnic at Hanging Rock* dramatises this and wisely refuses to solve the mystery of *how* or *why* the girls disappeared. Similarly, the Australian public refused to accept the conviction of Lindy Chamberlain for the murder of her daughter Azaria as a solution of this mystery. The controversy's deeply contradictory nature emerged dramatically in 1986, when, four years after her conviction, Lindy Chamberlain was freed without the original murder verdict being reversed. Whatever evidence forensic scientists may discover in the future, the Australian folk belief will prefer to link Azaria's disappearance with the benevolent/malevolent spirit of the Rock rather than 'solve' the enigma with a rational explanation. Such a folk belief may not be as explicit as the Greek legend of the Sirens, but it is fundamentally similar: it is both an attraction and a threat. So the Rock is consistently referred to as essential viewing for every Australian and for every visitor to Australia, yet descriptions of its attractiveness mingle with adjectives such as 'eerie' and 'mysterious'; photographs alternately show it benign and beautiful under the blue Australian sky, and threateningly red, purple or black under heavy cloud or darkening sky; descriptions of the magnificent view from the top are tempered with warnings that those with weak hearts should not attempt the climb.

These contradictory meanings of the Rock are at one with the contradictory meanings of Aboriginality for, in the mythology of tourism, the two become almost indistinguishable. The Aborigine is a personification of the central Australian landscape: each is equally and similarly opposed to the urban lifestyle of the typical white Australian.

The most insulting, white-centred meanings see Aborigines and their culture as objects of white spectacle. In the Sheraton foyer, all you have to do is 'Just ask, and a tour to see the dramatic Aboriginal rock paintings is yours', and a postcard on sale there shows Aborigines who, in the words of its caption, 'perform an ancient ceremony'. Words like 'perform' and 'dramatic' are disguised metaphors of theatre and carry with them the idea of a white 'audience' being 'entertained'. This effectively dislocates Aboriginal art from its own cultural context of ritual and spiritual significance and relocates it in a white world of spectacle. Similarly, in Alice Springs, at the Diamond Springs Casino Amphitheatre, every Friday night at 8 p.m. is a performance of 'Traditional Central Australian Aboriginal Corroborees as have been performed for centuries. Tickets available at the door, Adults $8.00, Pensioners $7.00, Children $5.00'. It is provocative to reverse the racial roles and imagine, for example, RSL veterans performing the Anzac Day ceremony weekly in a casino amphitheatre to entertain paying black spectators.

The tourist can choose from a number of 'Dreamtime and Namatjira Tours' and can, for example, pay $46 to 'spend half a day with Aboriginal people in their traditional environment; watch Aboriginal people making and using weapons and implements; find bush tucker and see how witchetty grubs are found, sample some after being cooked in warm ashes; sample bush cake and billy tea; learn about Aboriginal life.'

The impossibility of achieving all this in the four and a half hours that the tour takes is acknowledged in the slogan on the advertising material 'It takes a lifetime to understand an Aboriginal. The 'Dreamtime Tour' is a beginning'. This at least offers the contradictory possibility that the white spectator may not merely marvel at the difference, but may realise that the difference need not be understood from a position of white power and knowledge but may be more fully understood from a position of mutual respect.

Similarly, when Aboriginal people are described, as they often are, as a 'stone age' culture, there can be little doubt that the main meaning is a patronising white one in which a 'developed' civilisation looks back at the stage it evolved from: Aborigines are preserved (white) pre-history, our primitive ancestors caught in a time loop, whose continued existence celebrates the distance we have come. But there is also a contradictory sense in which our 'progress' is not seen as so unequivocally good. The white awe at the 'timelessness' of the Rock and of Aboriginal culture evidences a distrust of progress, a sense that it is taking us further away from our 'nature' rather than closer towards the perfect society. There is a sense that history is out of human control, is sweeping white society helplessly along with it, and that there is much to admire or even envy in a 'timeless' culture that has resisted this tide.

Conversely, of course, there is the sense that white Australia has a worryingly short history, and this is, in some way, compensated for by the enormously long history of the land and its Aboriginal inhabitants. The eternal present in which the ancient land and Aboriginal cultures are seen to exist becomes an instant history for the white Australian tourists, replacing the very different and less 'natural' European history that they have dissociated themselves from. The search for a national identity necessarily involves a search for a history.

While tourism certainly effaces the conflict between white and black in Australian history, it does offer some more positive meanings of Aboriginality than those circulated in the domains of economics, politics and law and order. In leaving these more 'workaday' domains behind, the tourist is open to more progressive understandings of Aboriginality than are ordinarily available in the white suburbs.

For whatever meanings of Aboriginality are current in any domain they are always constructed in opposition to meanings of white society. Aborigines are what whites are not. Sometimes this difference is seen as a threat, but sometimes, as in tourism, it can be seen as a compensation, as a means of liberating whites from the limitations of the society they have built and of offering them alternative ways of thinking.

The limitations of white urban society, symbolically as well as geographically on the fringe of the nation, underlie the awe at the vastness and emptiness of Australia's centre. The more crowded and confining our cities appear, the greater the significance of the empty interior. The more static and settled they appear, the less they are able to bear meanings of development and freedom. Being on the move symbolises the freedom which Australians see as their natural birthright. It is a common dream of many working couples to celebrate their retirement, their release from work, by a caravan trip around the continent. In exploring the nation, we are exploring ourselves.

The Ayers Rock Sheraton once again appeals to and helps construct this sense in another of its brochures:

> It's early morning, in the cool of the desert. Set in a timeless land lies the world's mightiest monolith—Mystique, Legend and an eerie magnetism surround Ayers Rock—9 km around 340 metres high beckoning all as a new day dawns.
>
> Nearby, the mystical Olgas, equally sacred to the Aboriginals and their ancestors. Rich in dreamtime folklore it is also a highlight of the sacred Uluru (Ayers Rock–Mt Olga) National Park.
>
> Across a thousand miles of severe and uncompromising desert the breeze travels before whispering into the splendour and magnificence of the Sheraton Ayers Rock Hotel, shaded by giant sails—a unique feature of this desert resort.
>
> As the breeze cools the full-sized tennis courts, shimmies the surface of the free form swimming pool, goes unnoticed in the spa it then travels another thousand miles to the east coast.

The breeze is a metaphor for the tourist, naturalising his or her free journey across the heart of the country before finishing back in civilisation on the east coast. The breeze may play in the Sheraton, but its real significance lies in its travels on either side, for it is in travelling the land that the Australian is most 'Australian'.

The Ugly Australian

The Australian tourist within Australia has been less actively mythologised than the Australian abroad. Australians have been making the ritual trip back to the cultural centre—Europe and especially England—from the beginnings of white settlement. The readiness with which successive generations of Australians have entertained thoughts of touring Europe in preference to touring Australia has been used as an example of the cultural cringe for almost as long. The relationship between Australian tourists and the country they are visiting, then, has always been one in which the discourses of nationalism are involved. For the generation who grew up in the 1950s and 1960s, the working holiday in Europe was customary rather than exceptional, and this practice has been inscribed in a rich and detailed recycling of the original nationalist myths of what it is that constitutes an Australian.

Such myths also surround earlier groups, such as the 'six bob a day tourists' of the AIF during the First World War. In *The Australian People and the Great War*, Michael McKernan described how the AIF were initially welcomed as heroes in Britain in 1916. By the end of the war, however, more traditional views had prevailed and the Australian soldiers were constructed as criminals, barred from many hotels and restaurants and dance halls. By the 1970s many expatriate Australians had become part of English culture; but the visibility of a Barry Humphries, a Richard Neville or a Germaine Greer did little to renovate the image of Australians. For every Joan Sutherland we produced, there seemed to be an *Oz* editor on trial. Richard Neville seemed to reinforce the iconoclastic, larrikin image; the first performances of David Williamson's plays were shockingly brutal in their language; and there was always the potential of Ian Chappell's Australian cricket team to redefine Australianness in opposition to the British. During the 1970s many expatriates reinforced common British perceptions of Australian culture. Germaine Greer was a regular source of cultural criticism of her home country, Barry Humphries' comic strip, *The Adventures of Barry McKenzie*, was read by the British as a critique of the ugly Australian, although Australians could see it as a scourge of British effeteness. Australian painters, writers, musicians and playwrights may have been applauded by the press back home, but the dominant images of Australians in the British press would be composed of the larrikin behaviour of Dennis Lillee and Jeff Thomson, or the regular stories about gangs of Australian shop-lifters, drugdealers and thieves.

The Australians travelling in Britain in the 1960s and 1970s encountered a large number of people to whom Australians were a familiar breed. But they also found themselves constructed within a very narrow and specific range of signifiers of Australianness: images from the past and from the quirky flora and fauna dominated—convictism, kangaroos, spiders. (Admittedly, these images were not helped by such moves as selling bad Australian port under the label 'Emu Port' or Australian claret under the label 'Kangarouge'.) This hostile displacement of Australia as a culture, as a society with an identity which involved more than just a liberal supply of sunshine, seemed almost conscious. Jokes about Australia's supposed lack of civilisation were in circulation then, and now. A British visitor to Australia as recently as three years ago amused the waiting press corps with a question: 'What is the difference between yoghurt and Australia?' The answer: 'Yoghurt has a culture.' In conversation one could be told that Australia was the only culture to pass from barbarism to decadence without going through civilisation on the way. It was in response to such a constant barrage of provocation that the ugly Australian abroad emerged.

Of course, there may well have been many denizens of Kangaroo Valley—the Australian-dominated section of Earls Court in London—who would have behaved in the crude and offensive manner of the mythic Australian tourist without such provocation. One of the interesting aspects of the Australian experience in England, however, is how many found themselves behaving in such a manner almost in spite of themselves. The range of British assaults on Australian national pride—deprecating remarks about our past, our present, our films, our wine—tended to touch those who had never seen themselves as in any way nationalistic before. A sense of indignation against the British was pervasive, and it was reinforced by the fact that this British insistence on their cultural superiority came at a time when the Australian tourists saw themselves as the bearers of a new national maturity and self-confidence.

Personal experiences can serve as cultural evidence, although as texts they are hard to 'fix' and read. Two of the authors had the experience of being an Australian in Britain during this period, and some of their experiences are illustrative. Graeme Turner continually felt rejected and alien despite his British parentage and an interest in British culture from his earliest years, ranging from the literature to the football to an addiction to *Beano*. Despite being successful in his postgraduate studies at an English university, he was told on a number of occasions that he had a personal defect in not having been to an English public school. The rigid British class system constructed an uncongenial place for him as an Australian and as a student. No matter how many times he was introduced to staff members, they would not recognise him in the corridors on the following day. (Admittedly, the University of Sydney had given him some foretaste, as a product of its Anglophilia, but this was mitigated by the attitudes of younger staff.) Most disconcerting, given the patronising view taken of Australia and Australians, was the degree of ignorance about it and them. One of Graeme's close friends, a graduate in art and history, eventually admitted she was surprised to find that Australians could *do* degrees at home. The sum total of her knowledge of Australian educational opportunities came from a television program on the 'School of the Air'.

It was the combination of strongly held opinions and basic ignorance that was most galling for Graeme and for many other Australians. Particularly when it was understood that the British had nothing *against* Australians really. Their attitudes to Australians were part of a wider complex of British nationalism and its Victorian ideology, affecting attitudes to the colonies and to Europe. As is the case with all nationalisms, the British saw Australian nationalism as a kind of blindness, while British nationalism was obviously justified or at least endearing. This did not mean that in arguments between British and Australian nationalists the British always remained aloof and unthreatened. During the 1974 Commonwealth Games, Graeme's British flatmate was goaded into totalling the separate medal tallies of England, Scotland and Wales to prove Britain's superiority to Australia in athletics and to explain the apparent superiority Australia had gained over England. Australians tended to relish moments when British nationalism was attacked by the same doubts and defended with the same lack of logic that Australian nationalism suffered under British scrutiny. England's failure to qualify for the 1974 World Cup in soccer rankled, and the fact that it was due to a defeat by Scotland hurt even more. Even as the finals proceeded, one of Graeme's English friends insisted that despite their defeat England was a better side and should have been included. The fact that Australia *had* made it, and was demonstrably a poor side, provided great opportunities for cultural exchanges.

Such tales easily become rancorous in the telling. However, the paradox of the ugly Australians in Britain of the 1970s was how much they wanted to be accepted by their hosts. An obstacle, for both sides, was the mixture of the familiar and the unfamiliar in the surroundings for the Australians, and in the Australians for the British. Feeling sufficiently nostalgic about the 'home country' to want to be accepted as honorary Englishmen, yet feeling sufficiently estranged by the nature of the society—its class structure, its obsessive orderliness (the image of queueing), its faintly ridiculous assurance of its role as a world power—Australians in England developed a deep ambivalence. The refusal of the English to accept Australians as 'part of the family' (unless as delinquent children) was countered by Australians' sense of the surprising strangeness of the family and its patterns of behaviour. It was not something that could be easily discussed with the British. Remarks about pub opening hours would be met by invocations of six o'clock closing, and the Australian would be forced on to the back foot yet again. The comparative strangeness of the English attitude to pets was something Graeme Turner never came to terms with. Perhaps this was due to his first encounter with a most exaggerated example: in his first three weeks in England he stayed with a couple who used to fill the bath every Friday night, pop a little weed in it, and allow their goldfish to 'take a walk'.

The ambivalence organised itself into deeply contradictory attitudes to English and Australian culture. On one side of the contradiction we had the deference to English culture—which is after all a central if paradoxical element in Australian nationalism. On the other side was the strong perception that, unlike Australia, England was a place with a past rather than a future. Many saw it as decadent and insular. Often this contradiction was addressed through crude and insulting behaviour—the loud complaints about warm beer in pubs, for instance—and the exaggerated adherence to rituals of Australian nationalism as both a defence against, and an offence to, the British. Because the main British complaint against the Australians was their lack of civilisation, behaving in a civilised manner was an act of betrayal. The response was thus vigorously uncivilised, even from women who found that a well-delivered expletive created a pleasing shock wave in British male company. Australia was constructed by such behaviour as a land of some difference, at least. It might be peopled by savages, but they were unrepentant savages, and they had come to be that way from dealing with a harsh and hostile environment. Few Australians resisted the opportunity to tell hugely inflated yarns about spiders, snakes, or the horrors of the outback. That they were simply recycling existing myths and constructions mattered less than the growing respect they could see on the faces of their hitherto sceptical audience. Inevitably, the conventional signifiers of nationalism surfaced. The lyrics of 'Waltzing Matilda' sprang to lips which had probably never uttered them outside a school room; moonlight flits, shoplifting, and minor circumventions of government systems became nationalist acts in which criminality was, ironically, a signifier of Australianism once again; disrespect for British authority and order was represented through such institutions as the campervan market that occupied the parking meters outside Australia House.

The ambivalence was resolved in other ways, too; by crossing the cultural floor to become an honorary Pom by denying and living down one's Australianness. Intellectuals, in particular, found it necessary to denigrate Australia in order to indicate a fitness for British life, and many returned with English accents, English manners and a veneer of cultural superiority to their native country, where an Anglophile establishment had a place ready for them. The result for this type was that their Australianness became invisible, leaving only the 'ugly Australian' to carry the national meaning.

The ugly Australian became a recognisable type, at least partly because it was impossible to be Australian and not be seen as ugly in some way or another. The colonised visited the colonisers and found that their ability to afford the trip, their vision in *wanting* to take it, had no effect on their colonial status. The response was to strike back, to terrorise the hosts with their own battery of images of Australianness, to ritualise and exaggerate them. So, when the film *The Adventures of Barry McKenzie* was shown in London, many Australian Londoners used it as a moment to celebrate rather than criticise the Australian abroad. Groups of Australians entered the cinema with cans of Fosters on board, looking forward to an hour and a half of vivid Pom-bashing. That this did little to change or even complicate English attitudes to Australians did not seem to matter much. What did matter was that it was a successful act of defiance, of asserting independence through the only terms available.

The ugly Australian in Britain was not simply the expression of a native Australian unpleasantness. It was a product of dominant constructions of the Australian in Britain as well as dominant constructions of the British in Australia; that is, it emerges from the relationships between the two countries rather than from the gratuitous impulses of one. And of course, the ugly Australian is not the only construction of the Australian overseas. It is the most *specifically* Australian, however, because those tourists who do not fit this image tend not to signal their Australianness either. The ugly Australian is created by a response to the specific difference of the new context overseas, which mobilises certain aspects of nationalist ideology to assert what becomes a lack of respect for those differences. In its more recent formations, Australians in Asia, it can be racist and, in its turn, colonising. For the Australians in Britain, it should not surprise us that the ugly Australian should take its most radical form when confronted with a context in which Australianness was both a subordinated and a delinquent discourse.

7 Monuments

In this book we have been trying to redress a balance, by drawing attention to popular currents within Australian culture which are often ignored or dismissed. But it's also necessary to recognise official culture's contribution to Australian culture, which offers its own powerful and persuasive definition of Australia. Pivotal here is a set of public monuments, which are typically massive and difficult to ignore. The word 'monument' comes from a Latin word meaning to warn or advise. Monuments exist to give lessons from the past to the present. Normally these are oppressive, threatening messages, death speaking to life. They tend to be heavy, impressive rather than beautiful. The word 'monster' comes from the same Latin root, and many monuments are monsters, deformed by the weight of significance they carry. If it's difficult to ignore them, it's equally inappropriate to like them.

In Praise of the Past

War memorials occupy a central place in the version of history offered by official culture through its monuments. This version of history is a foundation myth, a narrative which serves to legitimate the present order. Many other societies have had myths serving this function. As one instance from high culture, we mention for purposes of comparison Virgil's *Aeneid*, a monument in the written language. This work was written to justify the Augustan regime which had just won a bloody civil war, and to legitimate the Roman state which had just imposed the 'Roman peace' on the heartland of European culture in Greece and the Middle East. Augustus's right to rule went back only as far as his success in the battle of Actium, and Rome had been a power in the Middle East for only a hundred

137

years. Virgil's epic provided Augustus with a fake genealogy going back seven centuries, and he displaced the crucial battles from bloody victories in the present to equally bloody defeats in the past, at Troy, (in the Middle East). What Virgil knew as ideologue was that conquest provides a problematic basis of right, because it invites another act of attempted conquest in riposte, obliging the conquerors to remain armed and never at rest.

White Australia's problematic basis of right is handled not by Virgil but by silence. Like Rome, Australia was founded by an act of conquest, and the right of white Australians to their land derives ultimately from this. In a series of invasions the original inhabitants were driven from their lands, shot and poisoned, raped and plundered, in a war that was never declared and therefore cannot be officially ended. White Australia now treats Aboriginal Australians better, and various kinds of land rights legislation tacitly acknowledge part of the Aboriginal cause—although it is yet to be seen if they will do a great deal to address it. There is still no treaty of the kind that many Aborigines demand, which would at last acknowledge that there was a war, even though the terms of it would also concede that the Aborigines were defeated. White Australia is ready to accept economic or political responsibility, perhaps, but not guilt.

The beginnings of our nation, made concrete in monuments throughout the country, are placed elsewhere: in the Australian sacrifices in two European wars, and in the sufferings of the pioneers in their battle against a hostile nature (a concept that often incorporates hostile Aborigines as natural hazards like drought, flood and fire). The coming of age is at Anzac Cove, and the Anzac myth has proved remarkably durable. Where other nations celebrate victories, Australia celebrates what is paradoxically acknowledged to be a pointless and bloody episode fought on foreign soil on behalf of the colonial power. Its most obvious lessons would seem to be the futility of war and the self-interest (and inefficiency) of British imperialism—along with the naivety of those Australians who supported Australia's involvement in that war.

Such lessons were in fact learnt from the beginning by many of the troops themselves, and within the wider culture they can now be seen inscribed into such television programs as *Anzacs*. Where Gallipoli is seen in this way, the Australians emerge as even more embattled and heroic—the stoic indices of the 'coming man' inheritors (but not perpetuators) of a class-ridden and anachronistic old world. Anzac Day has survived the gradual emergence of the unofficial histories of Gallipoli and has proved a remarkably successful occasion for reinforcing a sense of national solidarity. The selectiveness with which history is mined for its myths, however, is revealed in the relative invisibility of another pointless and humiliating military adventure some 50 years later: in Vietnam not Turkey, and in support of American not British interests.

The ways in which history is mobilised to construct and sustain a mythology are complex; the least one can say is that they are motivated and determined by ideology rather than a disinterested search for an objective 'truth'. The result is always the same; the national past becomes a chain of events, progressively and inevitably delivering us into the present and, in so doing, making sense of it. To conflate the national history with the national character is to propose an organic connection between the two; our history is both a producer and product of what we are—our very 'nature'—rather than of the actions and interests of specific men, women, groups and classes. The national past is thus constructed as nature, not history, and the official monuments to its key moments are important participants in this process.

The 'text' we are going to read combines all of these elements—history, nature, and the national past—in its forms. Kings Park in Perth, dominating the skyline in that city, contains both a war memorial and a memorial to the pioneers, set in a context that weaves them together with other representative structures of meaning. As a park, and as a version of history, Kings Park is particularly popular and successful, with basic forms and meanings that can be found in every major Australian city.

The publicity material for Kings Park gives the general context, and the key terms through which it is grasped:

> Some sections of Kings Park have scarcely altered since it was dedicated for public recreation in 1872. A natural bushland of almost one thousand acres (403 hectares), Kings Park overlooks the Swan River and as well as picnic, sports and recreational facilities, it features a stunning botanic garden designed to display the wildflowers and native plants for which the State is renowned. The Botanic Gardens situated on the Mount Eliza Bluff, have twelve hectares devoted to the cultivation of Western Australian native flora as well as gardens devoted to the propagation of Californian, Mediterranean, South African and Eastern States plants. Exotics have been planted in the older, formal garden areas. The

extensive bushland so close to the metropolitan area, is the main park in a city which boasts one of the highest percentages of open space of any city in the world. It has links with the explorers and first settlers and with the native inhabitants before the area was settled by Europeans. When Captain James Stirling surveyed the Swan River in March, 1827 the crew obtained fresh water from the spring now called Kennedy Fountain at the foot of Mount Eliza. The early settlers also drew water here from 1829 onwards. The Park and Botanic Gardens are freely open at all times throughout the year, and even the briefest visit at night will reward you tenfold. The fairyland panorama of the City of Perth lights, the Narrows Bridge and the Swan River combine with the scents and sounds of the bush to create an atmosphere of mystery and delight.

The popular Kings Park Garden Restaurant, which has a licensed restaurant and a light snack bar, offers first-class dining facilities in a unique and breathtaking setting.

In this description two pairs of categories that we have seen before help to organise the meaning: nature–culture and past–present. They are paired so that nature becomes the past, culture becomes the present, but the terms are not held in total opposition. Our natural past is seen in the 'native' surroundings, reminding us of the original inhabitants (but not of their dispossession) as well as the struggles of the pioneers. There is another kind of nature, though; the European 'formal gardens' which are signifiers of culture's supremacy over nature. The recalling of the past is nostalgic, memorialising it in order to celebrate the rites of passage which culminate in the present. It is a complex text, and this is because the park serves such a unifying function, dissolving boundaries between Britain and Australia, white and Aboriginal, present and past, and even two opposing conceptions of history—the linear history of European culture and our own organic history of the land, nature.

This naturalising of history is made explicit in one 'monument' in Kings Park. This is a cross-section of a Californian redwood with its rings labelled with key historical moments. The history is essentially one of white military and colonial expansion, so the growth of white imperialism. Its Californian origin tells the same story—America simply provides an older instance than Australia of the 'natural' spread of European control and another example of the exclusion of the original inhabitants from the history of the nation.

Tree 'monument' in Kings Park, Perth.

The recorded and naturalised history:

Tree germinated	1187
Magna Carta	1216
End of Crusades	1288
Battle of Crecy	1346
Battle of Agincourt	1415
Invention of printing	1452
Columbus discovers America	1492
Dirk Hartog lands in WA	1616
Abel Tasman's voyages	1642
Great Fire of London	1666
Fleming discovers Swan River	1697
First settlement of Sydney	1788
Settlement of Swan River	1829
Foundation of Kings Park	1872
Federation of Australia	1901
Tree felled	1965

Memorial in Esplanade Gardens, Fremantle

Inscription:

This monument was erected by C.J BROCKMAN as a fellow bush wanderer's tribute to the memories of PANTER, HARDING and GOLDWYER, earliest explorers after Grey and Gregory of this terra incognita, attacked at night by treacherous natives, were murdered at Boola Boola near le Grange Bay on the 13th November 1864. Also as an appreciative token of remembrance of MAITLAND BROWN, one of the pioneer pastoralists and premier politicians of this State. Intrepid leader of the Government search and punitive party. His remains, together with the sad relics of the ill fated three recovered at great risk and danger from the lone wilds repose under a public monument in the East Perth Cemetery. Lest We Forget.

Greetings from
Kings Park
Perth W.A.

WAR MEMORIAL

Kings Park, Perth. The barbecues and paddling pools are of natural stone, and haphazardly ('naturally') arranged, but they're as safe and well controlled as a suburban backyard. Fire and Water are as far from their natural, dangerous state as possible. The giant karri is equally unsure whether it celebrates the grandeur of nature or man's ability to destroy it and chop it into equal pieces for easy transportation. Its living history of 363 years (almost twice that of the white man in Australia) is frozen at its transformation into a museum specimen, an uncomfortable monument to man and nature and their ambiguous relationship.

The explicit and offensive racism of the memorial in the Esplanade Park, Fremantle, to three explorers may be ideologically more acceptable in that it openly celebrates the racial conflict which is made invisible in the history constructed by Kings Park.

The Kings Park War Memorial (opposite) is both a specific structure and a pervasive presence in the park. First, the specific structure. There is nothing natural about *it*; the obelisk is a defiant asserting of man's power, not over nature but over other men. Its signification of power is to justify the sacrifices of the dead by proclaiming the solidity and permanence of the nation they fought for. The main entrance to the park leads to the monument as to a final destination, and the paths and flowerbeds are designed to also lead the eyes and feet towards this dominating structure. But its power is not certified by boundaries of the park, for the monument is on the highest point of Perth from which the city and river can be seen and ideally processed and which, in its turn, can be seen from points all over the city. The monument is, literally, a dominant point of view from which to make sense of both the history and the present Western Australia. The cultural dominance of this white, male, colonising history is expressed in the geographical dominance of the obelisk which embodies it.

It is common practice in Australia to place war memorials in parks or nature. This is different from European practice, as in London, Paris or Rome, whose war memorials are in the middle of the city, surrounded by buildings, roads and traffic, with not a blade of grass or tree in sight. Kings Park goes further than most; the setting itself is like a giant memorial tablet laid on its side, because many of the trees that line the roads through the park have bronze plates commermorating the name of an individual soldier and imply that the tree was planted there at the time of his death. Here not only the national history is seen as part of a natural cycle of events; the individual death is too. The metaphoric identification between the individual and the nation is asserted; in their sacrifice and heroism the roots of the nation are to be found. Thus, heroism and sacrifice are part of our 'nature' in all senses of the word.

There is a second, more clearly subordinate, memorial in Kings Park which deals with the other aspect of our mythic history: the more recent Pioneer Women's Memorial. Whereas the War Memorial is a hard, angular phallus, the Pioneer Women's Memorial is a series of fountains in a gently curving lake. One does not need to be a semiotician to read the difference. The male memorial is set in a position of power, overlooking Perth and visible for kilometres. The feminine memorial is in a hollow surrounded by trees and has no view. It is a place to look at from close up, not to look from or be seen from afar; it is private, secluded, instead of public and highly visible.

Such contrasts clearly express gender stereotypes, common to other cultures beside Australia. What is significant here is that the problematic act of settling/invasion is associated with the feminine role of nurturing, suffering and serving. The memorial fountain is a response to progressive feminist histories, which have forced academic historians to recognise the role of women in Australian history and social life. At the same time it uses this concession to neutralise the even more disturbing fact of white expropriation of the land, carried out by a group of whites who included soldiers, missionaries and government officials as well as 'settlers', male and female.

In its own low-keyed way, Kings Park is a masterpiece of ideology. The complex messages are woven in so unobtrusively that users of the park almost stumble on them for themselves, while enjoying its many attractions. Barbecues, swings, bike-rides, walks, lakes, views, places for children, adolescents, adults of all ages— Kings Park deserves its popularity but these harmless pleasures are linked up in a wider structure of legitimation. The complicity of the populace is wooed, not demanded as in the more typical European war memorial, but that only makes it more effective. Virgil abandoned pastoral poetry to write his ideological epic, but Kings Park is a pastoral with an epic scope, carrying out the same political functions as the *Aeneid* with equal skill.

Art Galleries

Art galleries are another important class of monument, erected by governments as official contributions to Australian culture. Their more specific function is similar to war memorials: to intervene in the definition of that culture. They work in two main ways: as physical monuments and as authoritative arbiters of what art and culture are, through their selection and arrangement of the 'monuments' they contain. Official Australian culture, however, meets with popular resistance in both these areas, as our reading will try to elucidate. (Much of the following discussion draws on Copping and Turner's 1983 article, listed in our bibliography.)

There are two basic formats of art gallery in Australia, as in Britain: the traditional, and the modernist. The Art Gallery of New South Wales is the exemplary instance of the traditional type, while the Australian National Gallery in Canberra, and the Melbourne and Perth galleries, are examples of the modernist form. Although these two models seem very different in many important ways, there are limits to these differences; in many ways their meanings are the same. In the 1980s as much as in the 1880s, Australian art gallery architecture expresses an almost equal subservience to external, international taste.

So the New South Wales building is no more of an anachronism now than when it was built. One need only look at it to see that it was never meant to speak of an indigenous culture; rather its function was to participate in that culture's colonial reverence for a European past. It has a neoclassical facade of monumental proportions, which already had a long history of allusions: to the British museum and behind that to Italian retreads of Roman retreads of Greek originals. It alludes also to the country mansion of the British aristocrat who used it to insert himself into that history. The result is a declaration of the culture's subscription to a tradition which has continued unbroken for over two millennia, as the standard of excellence. This declaration may or may not be accepted, because the traditions invoked are so obviously constructed. The exterior walls have inscribed on them the names of European masters—Raphael, Titian, and so on—but the gallery within has virtually none of their works.

The New South Wales art gallery is part of a chain of texts. It is set in a grassed park called 'The Domain', the name recalling the 'demesne' of the English country house. In nineteenth-century Britain the growth of the urban working class threatened the traditional aristocracy. As a strategy to defend itself against charges of exclusiveness and to signal a democratisation of its privileges, the aristocracy produced 'democratic' versions of its culture. Thus public art galleries and libraries were created, housed in imitation country mansions like the private collections they imitated. Similarly, public parks imitated the private parks of the great landowners. However, the Art Gallery of New South Wales, in its pseudo temple-mansion, signals its upper-class tradition more effectively than the attempt to democratise it. On the other hand, the Domain, like Kings Park, is bustling with populist activity, with its Sunday afternoon speakers and its open-air concerts. The democratisation

of the Domain is unencumbered by the elitist pretensions of 'official' Australian culture and its highbrow definitions of art. So, paradoxically, it is able to present performances of opera to huge audiences. The gallery's populism is less convincing. The publicity brochure for its Art Gallery Society uses the headline 'It's your gallery, make the most of it', trying to provoke the general populace to an equivalently brash social activity. But it is the Art Gallery Society's exclusiveness that is the major lure—the brochure offers 'inside' benefits, 'private' collections and, of course, 'new friends', unlike those common people out there on the Domain.

The Domain itself is part of a series of spaces running from north to south. To its north is the Botanic Gardens. Along the west, are the New South Wales library, Parliament House, Sydney Hospital, the Royal Mint and Hyde Park Barracks museum, and the law courts. This array of State power, opposite the art gallery, offers it support. To the south is the Victorian gothic Catholic cathedral, St Mary's. Further south is Hyde Park, divided in two by Park Street, with the Archibald Memorial Fountain in one half, and the 'pool of remembrance' and Anzac Memorial in the other. This set of texts affects the meaning of this art gallery, and a similar context affects the meaning of the National Gallery of Victoria in Melbourne. On its own, juxtaposed to the Domain, the New South Wales gallery might be read as isolated, vulnerable, alien and out of date. As one of a series of texts expressing different aspects of State power, its archaic claims to authority cannot be so easily dismissed, or enjoyed.

The other kind of art gallery in Australia is the aggressively modern kind. The new Australian National Gallery in Canberra is the major representative of this type. Its elegant gleaming abstract forms seem far removed from the darkened neoclassical motifs of the New South Wales gallery. It doesn't declare its allegiance to any past; there are no allusions; it doesn't declare any Great Tradition as the prerequisite for entering it. It thus seems more egalitarian.

There are a number of ways in which this appearance is misleading. First, the context for appreciating the National Gallery in practice includes other art galleries, even though examples of them are not directly present. Part of the meaning of the National Gallery is that it's *not* like the New South Wales or similar galleries, and not like the British Museum or the National Gallery in London. The apparent lack of history signified by the Australian National Gallery is in practice a very specific history, in which an older obsession with the past has been transcended by a modern rejection of it, and its colonial status.

The National Gallery asserts another connection, however, which exists in the concrete present. It is part of a complex of public buildings, around the huge artificial lake named after Walter Burley Griffin. Its general style is similar to the new Supreme Court building, just as the New South Wales art gallery mirrored the forms of the Parliament building. So although it is unmistakably modern, it still claims the same kind of allegiance with State power. It is its cultural arm, drawing on the same sources of

GETTING IT RIGHT

Australia has pretty much got its new National Gallery right.
Other approaches might have worked. But quality undoubtedly distinguishes
the present shape of the collection and its presentation.

The success of the Australian National Gallery, which officially opens
on October 12, is in marked contrast to the neglect of much of the material
in the National Archives and the National Library.
The National Gallery provides an excellent model of what is possible.

On page 4 of this special National Times colour magazine, the director
of the Victorian Gallery, Patrick McCaughey, gives a lively introduction to som
of his favourite works in the Canberra gallery. On page 25, staff writer
Phillip McCarthy traces the history of the new gallery and the development
of the philosophy behind the collection.

The transparencies for the reproductions used in the magazine were supplied by
the National Gallery. Layout is by National Times staff designer Dean Boyce.

COVER: This jade Olmec mask from Mexico, dating from
between 800 and 300 BC is part of the Australian National
Gallery's fine pre-Columbian central American collection.

authority, arousing (for those who resist) the same antagonism. Its placement in Canberra, distant from where 'ordinary' Australians live, tells the same story. In spite of appearances, nothing much has changed in the positioning of art galleries in relation to the State.

Context contributes decisively to the overall meaning of a public monument. The Art Gallery of Western Australia is a modern building, like the National Gallery. But unlike the National Gallery, the New South Wales gallery, or the Melbourne gallery, it can't generously offer the public any signs of a democratic purpose. Instead of a grassy Domain, it has its own meagre grounds, brick paving surrounding an artificial pond and fountain. All too visibly around it is the grimy and run-down cityscape of the suburb of Northbridge, a notorious trouble spot patrolled by police over the weekends but now being transformed and tamed by a massive cultural complex. The art gallery, built close to the existing museum, has quickly been followed by the huge Alexander Library which equally imperiously imposes an official state culture upon the ethnic subcultures for whom the area was previously home. The art gallery and library have been deliberately set apart from the rest of their urban surroundings, elevated above those who approach them. A long brick-paved walk leads to the gallery and maximises the opportunities to receive the building's scale and substance and to forget the surrounding area. Other public monuments, Parliament House or the law courts or war memorials, are too far away to be included in the immediate reading of this gallery, so it is their distance that is signified instead. This art gallery is not so closely linked to the protecting power of the State, but is aligned rather with an official definition of culture as the preservation of the great works of the past (and sometimes, the present).

The Western Australian gallery is like all galleries in signifying its exclusiveness, its distance from the average and the popular. In common with the New South Wales gallery and the Melbourne and Canberra galleries, the facade has an absence of windows and a disguised and discreet entrance which present us with a partially interrupted but almost featureless wall. In all these, it's hard to avoid a sense that this wall has been erected to protect something from us rather than to offer us a display of its contents. It certainly prohibits informal or casual entry. This meaning is inflected differently in the Western Australian gallery, whose greater insecurity is communicated brilliantly by the ambiguous sculpture that dominates the approach to the building. Gerhard Marck's 'The

The Queensland Art Gallery. Outside it is like Fort Knox, inside it is Versailles. Part of an arts complex on Brisbane's south bank (the comparison with London's South Bank is irresistible and is frequently invoked) the gallery has the formidable formal exterior of the Perth gallery discussed in the text. There are no informal outdoor restaurants taking advantage of the perspective across the river, and the gallery cafe is enclosed by high walls facing on to a decaying part of the city. On a Sunday afternoon there were fewer than 30 people in the building.

Caller' in some ways recalls an antique barker, calling customers to the gallery without distinction or favour. From this point of view we can read the stance as an egalitarian 'come ye all' open invitation, though this is in direct contradiction with the signals of exclusivity in the building itself.

Inside the entrance of all these galleries, new and old, the space is not unlike that of a temple or church, meant to be used by the faithful and approached with respect by the merely curious. The Western Australian gallery has an open area at the entrance, with a high steepled ceiling; the entrance to the Victorian gallery has a stained-glass ceiling (although much of the rest of the foyer resembles an expensive hotel); the old section of the New South Wales gallery directly recalls the decorations of ancient temples. In all, the sense of silence and space evokes the effect of entering a cathedral. This isn't peculiar to Australian galleries. Bourdieu and Darbel in

The interior of the Queensland Art Gallery is spectacular, displaying its architecture rather than its contents (this is just as well, for there are problems with its holdings). But it is the most imaginative of the new galleries in its interior design and thus falls into the paradigm of the palace or architectural folly rather than the bank or church. As a gallery this may not be appropriate, since the building is the subject of display, not its contents. As a Queensland government enterprise, it is more appropriate, since a spectacular gallery is more important than a spectacular collection.

L'amour de l'art cite statistics that show that of 66 per cent of French working-class respondents to the question 'what does an art gallery remind you of most' replied 'a church'. (John Berger's *Ways of Seeing* is the source here.) The sacred nature of these buildings is underlined in the Western Australian gallery by a small admonitory handout which is provided for visitors—something deemed unnecessary in most other galleries perhaps because the buildings themselves are more obviously serious: 'A gallery', it says, 'is a serious place for study, contemplation and pleasure...it is not a playground.' The order that places study and contemplation before pleasure highlights again the confusion between the myth of the open 'people's' gallery and the shaping myths of art itself. Art *does* discriminate between the classes. Pierre Bourdieu's work establishes that 'educated people are at home with scholarly culture', while the 'least sophisticated' find themselves in a position when confronted with such culture 'identical with that of the ethnologist who finds himself in a foreign society and is present at a ritual to which he does not hold the key'. To provide opportunities for 'study and contemplation' is to favour the kind of person who might wish to accept that opportunity and to institutionalise assumptions about the education and other kinds of cultural background that people might bring to the gallery. Such assumptions imply an elite. This elite becomes by architectural transformation the cultural 'elect' as we move inside the gallery and into the paradigm of the 'church of art'.

The monetary value of the artworks requires an additional cultural function of the contemporary gallery—in particular the modern ones—which is the function of a custodial institution, a bank or vault. While the interior offers an austere and puritanical version of the church, the exterior is that of a large financial institution, like Fort Knox, which confers on to the gallery the function of banking the State's cultural capital (the more the cognoscenti appreciate the paintings, the more the paintings appreciate as investments; once again the linguistic pun has a social and political dimension). The paintings are bullion, guarded by attendants dressed in uniforms like those of the police or army, rather than the robes of the church. Their function is not to present the paintings to us, but to guard them from us. There is a paradox here, of course, for the 'we' who have penetrated so far into the vaults of the culture are not the ones from whom the pictures need protection.

The art collections and their arrangement constitute the other major message system of art galleries. The content of this message system has two major themes in tension with each other: on the one hand, a definition of culture in general and the place in it of Australian culture; on the other, a version of history, again both a general and a specifically Australian cultural history. These definitions and versions of history have all the weight and authority that the State can give, yet there is always an incompleteness, a fragmentariness about the actual messages. The collections themselves are inevitably incomplete. They have always accumulated over time, and have depended on current tastes and budgets and the vagaries of successive purchasing policies. But a degree of incoherence and incompleteness in the message is itself a message: primarily about the marginality of art within Australian culture, precisely the factor that the art galleries most strenuously seek to overcome.

Given this central problem, it is the balance between Australian and European art that is most significant. At one extreme there is the view of Australian culture as irredeemably impoverished, as put so forcefully in 1935 by Professor Cowling, the Professor of English Literature at the University of Melbourne. Cowling attacked Australian life and literature for its lack of tradition. Australia had to recognise, he said, that literary culture was not indigenous but came from a 'European source'. Further, because there were no 'ancient churches, castles, ruins—the memorials of generations departed' Australian life was too lacking in depth to make first-class art. This conception would be vehemently denied now, and was controversial in the 1930s when it was first uttered, yet it still seems to underpin the purchasing policies of our art galleries, as an implicit and unacknowledged ideological premise.

The insistence on purchasing works by the 'great' names of a past European tradition is often carried to perverse lengths in Australian galleries. Occasionally this is justified by way of their importance for Australian artists (as occurs in the New South Wales gallery) rather than for their intrinsic merit. Sometimes the history is a non-British counterhistory, as in the case of the coverage of the New York School at Canberra. Because major works by major artists rarely come on to the market and are expensive when they do, our galleries have to be content with minor works and sketches, works that derive their significance from their relation to the major works—from which they are, of course, now separated. As resources for the serious art student, such acquisitions are of minimal value. Their function is to satisfy our cultural pretensions without ever challenging our egalitarian sentiments. They modestly deny that Australia is a cultural backwater by importing random samples of those elements of civilisation that we associate with the cultural richness of Europe: and the modesty itself cancels the denial.

Paradoxically, while Australian galleries look to the elite, aristocratic, European tradition to establish their terms of reference, the Australian art that they collect tends to be strongly nationalist, and thus more egalitarian, in content. Like their counterparts in fiction, drama, and latterly in film, the reputations of the artists of the Heidelberg School have benefitted from this. A significant number of our key paintings refer directly or indirectly to the myths of the bush which emerged from the nationalism of the 1890s. Russell Drysdale's 'Drover's Wife' refers inevitably to Henry Lawson's story, while 'Sofala' mythologises the rural past. Sidney Nolan's 'Ned Kelly' series not only renovates a national folk hero as material for high art but also explores the documentary and populist potential of his apparently abstract art in order to present it as cryptic narrative. While appearing to be demanding on the viewer, it isn't, and the representation of Kelly in his black mask becomes a 'logo' for the series and for a new confluence of populism and nationalism in Australian modern art.

There is one kind of gallery that points to a recurring fissure in Australian culture: galleries of Aboriginal art. In a traditional gallery this problem was invisible: Aboriginal art was displayed in a museum, not an art gallery. In a modern gallery this solution is not so easy, because Aboriginal art is gaining world recognition. This recognition from the centres of European culture, in America and Europe (though not, significantly, in Britain as yet) is troublesome to a confessedly provincial culture which defers to those centres. Aborigines' supposed lack of any culture was one of the justifications for their dispossession. If they can now produce (and have always produced) fine works of art, how can that dispossession now be justified? So where Aboriginal art is exhibited, it is framed, titled and provided with the name of artist (where possible) and date of purchase. It is, in other words, appropriated out of its own cultural context and turned into white art for white critical appreciation.

This is simply a higher-class version of the process we saw operating in the domain of tourism: making Aboriginal culture into art for white appreciation is fundamentally no different from making it into spectacle for white entertainment. But in both versions of the process, these are signs of respect that contradict the essential disrespect, signs of a desire to understand Aboriginal culture, albeit in white terms, that contradict the lack of understanding evidenced in the disregard for the effect of the cultural and physical context upon the meaning of a work of art. The unproblematic appropriation, hopefully less than total, of Aboriginal art into white official culture is a further sign of the displaced and mystified anxiety structured into our parks and war memorials, stemming from the injustice that is at the foundation of white Australian society.

But the art galleries of Australia should not be seen as the uncontested definers of art within Australian culture. Art reproductions are sold extensively by art galleries and others, and these flow round and beyond the patchy gallery collections. And popular culture develops its own Great Tradition. In an edition of the television quiz show, *Family Feud*, for instance, the audience was asked to name a famous artist. Names traditionally associated with the highpoints of art history dominated, with Michelangelo and Leonardo da Vinci among the first four names. More modern, but still well-established traditional names followed—Renoir, for example. But numbers two and three, respectively, were Rolf Harris and Larry Pickering. In a country where the argument between populism and high art is inextricably intertwined with the history of the arts' attempts to justify a role for themselves, this has some typicality. It highlights the problematic ways in which the Australian public sees art, the artist, and the ideological space reserved for both within the culture. The program's audience, in choosing Pickering and Harris as famous artists, seems to be insisting that there is not a vast difference between painting the roof of the Sistine Chapel with the legend of the Fall, and painting Larry Pickering's boatshed all the colours of the Berger rainbow.

Art in Australia is a privileged area, and one towards which the suspicion of privilege that marks other areas of Australian life has always been active. Artists throughout our history have complained of the philistines of Australia. Our censorship laws exposed us to ridicule from outside, and the caricature of Sir Les Patterson (Barry Humphries' cultural attaché to the Court of St James) draws his comic point from his lampooning of Australian pretensions to what Raymond Williams spells 'culchah' as ignorant and phony. In a culture as pragmatic and as physical as Australia, the artist was always going to have a hard time fitting in. The ideological effectiveness of art galleries and museums was never likely to rate alongside that of Kings Park.

The Sydney Opera House

Among the range of monuments contributed by the State to Australian culture there is at least one that is unequivocally a success: the Sydney Opera House. It houses operatic performances which count among the highest forms of high culture, yet it has entered profoundly into the popular imagination as a complex symbol of Australian identity. Other such symbols are either animals—kangaroos, koalas—or refractions of Aboriginal culture—boomerangs, or Ayers Rock. No other product of white European culture has achieved this status, none of the art galleries, war memorials, law courts or multistorey edifices that are scattered through Australia's cities. What is so special, and so significant, about it?

The *Sydney Morning Herald* editorial on the day the Opera House was officially opened by the Queen (20 October 1973) perceptively placed the moment in perspective by comparing it to the opening of the Sydney Harbour Bridge in 1932. The opening of the bridge was something of a landmark in the recovery of a society diminished by the depression, haunted by the spectre of war, and sliding into an exaggerated dependency on its 'great and powerful friends', the United States and Britain, in foreign policy and trade. The bridge, was, as the editorial points out, something of a 'parochial event', providing evidence of a 'provincial city's move into twentieth-century technology'. The bridge signifies industry and technology, its formal brutalism unashamedly mechanical, functional and practical. Even the addition of the pylons, introducing elements of a Tower Bridge shape in addition to the basic coathanger, failed to disguise the functional purity of its design. The Opera House, though, is a very different object.

The architect, Joern Utzon, is the focus of one set of myths about the building. Although a Swede, not an Australian, he represented a distinctive Australian type reborn: the pioneer, the dreamer, the man of vision battling against a blinkered bureaucracy and in effect tricking them into having a far more ambitious building than they wanted or deserved. The arguments about the escalating cost and time required for the completion of the building dominated the early days of its nineteen-year history of construction.

In addition to being too expensive, it has been seen as failing to fill its role as a concert hall complex. Acoustically, it is a disaster; Max Harris speaks for a large number of critics when he observes that it is 'extremely beautiful and enchanting. . . but it is a functional fiasco'. The original purposes of the halls within the complex were never met. Further, the performances within them are still primarily those aimed at an elite audience—ballet, opera, orchestral concerts, drama, dance—with the free outdoor concerts and light entertainment listed in the year's programs under the heading of 'other activities'. Paradoxically but importantly, it's precisely this lack of functionality that is valued, as an expression of egalitarian scepticism towards the high culture it serves so badly.

The Opera House is variously described as one of the 'wonders of the world', or a second 'Taj Mahal', making it a 'contribution to international culture', its magnificence 'belonging to the world'. Editorials on the opening in the *Sydney Morning Herald*, The *Australian* and The *Age* saw it as a 'triumph' (the *Age*) or a 'symbol and an achievement' (the *Herald*), and both the *Herald* and the *Australian* devoted special supplements to the occasion. The metaphors, descriptions and discourses used to represent it in 1973 seem to have stuck. The current brochure describes it as 'the eighth wonder of the world' and the 'greatest architectural adventure and achievement of modern times'. Peter Luck, nearly ten years later in his TV program *This Fabulous Century*, discusses the Opera House under the general episode heading of 'Australiana' and sees it as being 'like the pyramids' in that it is not 'so much a functional object but a decorative symbol'. He, too, calls it one of the wonders of the modern world, a phrase that is the most commonly used in references to the building. The source of this phrase, and of the reference to the pyramids, may actually be the Queen's opening address. The *Herald* reported her as saying, among other things:

> Controversy of the most extreme kind attended the building of the pyramids yet they stand today—4,000 years later—acknowledged as one of the wonders of the world. I hope and believe this will be so for the Sydney Opera House. The Opera House will have something the pyramids never had—it will have life.

She, too, dismissed the functionalist objections:

> . . . to express itself fully, the human spirit must sometimes take wings—or sails—and create something which is not just utilitarian and commonplace.

The 'wonder of the modern world' is anything but commonplace. Rather, it is 'a work of art in its own right', as the *Herald* called it, which is part of our artisitic heritage in 'exploiting what is unique in Australian experience' while also finding 'a place of importance . . . as part of international culture'. Like all great art, says the *Age*, 'the Opera House does not belong to Mr Utzon or to Sydney'; indeed, the Melbourne paper points out, 'it belongs to the world'. Seen in this way it is not surprising that Utzon's name is still connected with the building he abandoned halfway through construction; great art is created by artists, and the Opera House must have an author. Despite the New South Wales government's claim in its tourist handouts that the Opera House was built by the

OUTDOOR DANCING DISPLAY AT FOLKLORIC FESTIVAL

THE MAGNIFICENT CONCERT HALL

The Sydney Opera House.
The triumphant democracy
of its exterior ensures its easy
incorporation into the popular imagination: from tea
towels to T-shirts, its image
belongs to the people of
Australia. It's free and open
to all, a place for meeting, for
festivals and for being Australian. But the awesome
interior of the concert hall is
a cathedral of 'Art' whose
brow is as high as its vaulted
ceiling.

government, it is clearly Utzon's personal 'dream' or 'fantasy' we are expected to admire.

An interesting complication of this invocation of art and authorship in the newspaper treatments of its opening is the close coincidence with Patrick White's reception of the Nobel Prize for literature. Several papers carried articles on White in the same issue as their features on the Opera House. Although explicit connections were not drawn, the two items combine in constructing the image of the 1970s' renaissance in Australian culture, one of the abiding myths of the Whitlam era. The Opera House's contribution, though, is unique in that it does something new indeed, and allows Australians to see their culture as capable of creating monuments for the twentieth century in the way the Egyptians did for their era. Instead of a cultural backwater, the culture signified by the Opera House is a cradle of modern civilisation.

It is not surprising that the Opera House possesses a kind of uniqueness in the myths of Australia. Most of the texts examined in this book negotiate a relationship with those areas of Australian experience seen to be naturally distinctive—the land, the native animals, the pioneering history, the bush, and so on—by way of acculturating them, incorporating signifiers of the natural into a cultural and often urban context. We have looked at how the suburban home does this. Although there are many aspects of the structure of the Opera House which do invoke these myths—the colour of the pink granite, the topaz glass, the shadings of the tiles on the sails, the 'sails' themselves and their reflection of the Harbour's activities, even the basic dome shape which it shares with the Bridge and with Ayers Rock—it has carved out a different place for itself.

If the mark of the culture's imposition of itself on the natural environment is the architectural mode of featurism, then the Opera House is featurism elevated to the level of an artistic mode. Despite its close blending with the harbour, the Opera House is definitively man-made, 'inspired', conceived: a signifier of culture. Its representation may be cluttered with invocations of classical monuments, of the wonders of the world, of its consonance with an ancient classical architecture which symbolised the spirit and aspirations of its people, but it is nevertheless aggressively modern. Its dominant discourse is one of modernity, and its function for the culture now is as the primary signifier of the twentieth-century version of the new, confident, cosmopolitan Australia.

Oddly enough, it was commenced at a time of deep cultural cringe, but it was completed in the more nationalist days of Whitlam. The meanings it took on were those of the 1970s, not those connected with the days of its initial conception. Thus its function now is not simply to decorate the harbour but to present Australia to the world in the most positive fashion, as a leader in the modern, the contemporary and the unique. (The headline in the *Herald* stressed this function: 'Sydney has its day of glory . . . and the world watches', it said.) Rivalled by the Centrepoint Tower, preceded by the El Alamein fountain, but still the leader (since there are equivalent structures to Centrepoint elsewhere, and there were direct precedents for the fountain) the Opera House draws on its absolute self-indulgence, its total commitment to a signifying rather than a functional vision. Its addition of technological wizardry, its 'ahead-of-its-time' status as a feat of engineering and structural design, enables it to unite art and technology and thus establish itself as a building that is metonymic of the acme of twentieth-century architecture.

This is how it is seen outside Australia, and its importance within Australia rests partly on the way the world sees it. The *Australian*'s supplement on the opening included a feature on overseas reaction under the heading 'They love it or hate it—but they don't ignore it'. Not being ignored is a novelty indeed for Australian culture, and the affection with which the Opera House is regarded, particularly in Sydney, seems motivated at least in part by gratitude for this. The perceived marginalisation of Australia underlying the cultural cringe and the continual comparisons with the richer civilisations of Europe is halted by the very building which was conceived in envy of the cultural centres of Europe. Instead of institutionalising the glories of the European past, it asserts the manifest glory of the Australian present. The role of the Opera House in updating the Australian image is explicitly dealt with in an advertisement within the *Australian* supplement. In it, Australia's unique flora and fauna are seen as obsolete representatives of the nation. A picture of kangaroos appears as the nostalgic residue of the less confident past. The new Australia is no longer the location of odd, unevolved creatures, but of a 'perfect example' of the 'ingenuity of man'. Now, the advertisement asserts, we can see ourselves as having contributed to the 'forward cultural development of mankind'.

The Opera House is there to be looked at; it is an image, a signifier open to all. Aesthetic, modernist it may be, but it is also democratic and egalitarian. It has deliberately broken away from the signifers of class and tradition. It is not European and is therefore non-aristocratic. To understand its democracy we only need to move up the hill to compare it with the Art Gallery of New South Wales.

The democracy of the Opera House is partly in its design. Besides its subtlety and aestheticism there is also something vulgar, overemphatic and brash about it. It is spectacular, and the main source of its egalitarianism is its placement and exteriority. In becoming an image of Sydney, of Australia, it becomes the property of all; possessed by its lookers and photographers it is instantly and easily appropriated into popular culture; photographs, postcards, T-shirts, tea towels, glittery wall hangings, ashtrays, all the paraphernalia of mass accessibility. Our art galleries deny mass accessibility and suggest that what matters is *inside*, away from the public. Their severe exteriors, restrained and solid, offer no general invitation either to enter or to look but rather a challenge that only the initiated will accept.

But the Opera House is different, since what happens inside pales into insignificance beside its triumphant exteriority. The broad steps lead around it rather than into it. These steps, still not leading to the exclusive inside, occasionally act as the stage or amphitheatre for free public performances. The terrace that surrounds it is patrolled by lunchtime joggers, strollers and those who simply want to sit in the sun. The fact that the benches provided along the esplanade alternately face the building and the Harbour underlines the fact that it is a place to look *from* as well as *at*. Indeed, the formal entrance for the car-borne, who are, we assume, the traditional elite opera-goers, is positioned dingily beneath the steps, making the Rolls-Royced creep unseen to their expensive (but still subsidised) seats. Their exclusiveness, in a nice twist, *excludes* them from the general, public meaning.

A factor that must not be overlooked here is the simple one that the building *is* impossible to ignore; it does signify the existence of a particularly single-minded vision, and its every perverse and felicitous line flies in the face of the conventional corporate architecture we are used to seeing in our cities. A walk around the Opera House does involve the same kind of activities normally associated with a walk around the cultural centres of the great cities of Europe; one experiences the same blend of the familiar and unfamiliar, one looks the same way, receives its presence in the same way. In comparison to the civic architecture of most modern cities it is simply spectacular.

But it is more than this, for one does not only look at it, but also looks out from it, at those other great signifiers of Sydney, the bridge and the harbour. All three of these great images are accessible and open to all. The common comparisons of the Opera House to wings, sails, Ayers Rock, palm tree fronds, all link it to nature; we seem to want it to take on meanings of nature as much as those of culture. And that is its function in this great city-scape, to defuse the mythic contradiction between the bridge and the harbour. For nothing could be more man-made, more functional than the bridge, imposing itself over and defeating the natural gap between the south and north shores. And in the 1930s our conquest over the harsh Australian nature was a sign of our development and progress. In the 1950s and 1960s, however, we wish to harmonise our culture with the natural. The Opera House changes the meaning of the city-scape from man conquering nature to man working with nature.

The Opera House is far more than a sign of high Australian culture, which may help to explain the enormous contradictions embedded in its construction and in its place within Australian mythology. Within a culture that is dubious of the value of art, that suspects individualism and difference, that is pragmatic rather than idealist, the building seems to stand for everything that Australian life does not. And yet, contradictorily, as we have seen, it offers itself for democratisation. And it is in this paradox that we can find the secret of its appeal and its central place in the iconography of Australia. It is a giant exception that opened up space for new views of Australia at a time when the political system was also engaging in reform and redefinition. Unlike the reforms of the Labor Party, however, the Opera House managed to operate without threatening anybody. Its uselessness for the cultural buffs it was meant to serve saved it, enabling it to be read as a sign, a monument, rather than an elite institution. The nature of the sign inserts an element that is missing from most constructions of Australia—of radical modernity, individualist vision, and of the importance of abstract symbols in building a cultural identity. Its very otherness from dominant ideologies seems to be its credential. Clearly, if it was a more functional building it would not be such an important one. Equally clearly, it does now have use for millions, although not the use it was intended for. Its primary function is as a place, a symbol, not a concert hall, and it provides the reminder of potential not normally accepted as Australian: that of building a significant, not just prosperous, culture.

8   The Australian Accent

The Australian accent is one of the clearest markers of Australianness. Three words from the mouth of a Hoges, and we and the rest
of the English-speaking world know instantly where he comes
from. But as a badge of national identity the accent has some curious properties. Millions of Australian viewers laugh at Hoges on
TV, as though his kind of Australian belongs to a different species.
To some extent, they're right. Only about a third of Australians
speak like Hoges. The rest are more up-market Australians, whose
laughter marks their sense of superiority to this lower form of life.
But that's not all there is to it. Paul Hogan was named 'Australian
of the Year' in 1986. He has shown that his accent and style are not
only for home consumption: the Hoges package is a good export
commodity. In Britain it sells Fosters lager. In America it sells Australia itself. Non Australians, it's clear, listen and laugh, feel warm
and buy. The Australian accent is both unique yet internationally
recognisable, ridiculous but potent. It unites yet divides Australians
themselves. Understanding such paradoxes can go a long way
towards understanding the complexities and contradictions of
the Australian national identity and the processes by which it is
constructed.

'Accent' often refers just to the voice, to characteristic ways of
speaking a common language, but the word basically means an
emphasis. Just as there is an Australian way of producing the
sounds of English, there's an Australian way of doing many other
things, such as working and playing, eating and dressing. We call all
these part of an Australian accent, in a broader sense of the word.
They all work in the same way, through relative shifts against a
common standard, not an absolute difference. They all have a common function, to define an Australian identity. That identity has
the same complex and ambiguous relationship to everyday Austra-

lian life. And at the core of this definition of Australianness is a set of meanings quite important enough to make Paul Hogan the Australian of the year.

Hawkespeak: The politics of accent

NOW WE'LL ALL TALK IN REAL AUSSIE LINGO
Our vowels are slacker since we went into Labor

Ahh, goodday!

If I said to you that was Bob Hawke, you wouldn't find it hard to believe.

Since he became P.M. he's changed the language of Australia.

Don't you feel sorry for all those people who still say darnce, charnce and hom-o-sexual. The great strength of this Hawke-speak is that nobody feels embarrassed by others. O.K.

In respect of all the privately educated people whose vowels are impeccable, the only conclusion I can reach is that they are slightly out of tune with the sunburnt country.

You even get the impression that some of our liberal leaders, for instance, were educated out of the country.

Did Andrew Peacock go to Geelong Grammar, or Eton? You get my drift?

. . . There are so many Australians with the Hawke accent now that the tone and accents of the exclusively educated seem out of kilter with the nation.

What better or more appropriate greeting to the returning Aussie than 'goodday mate' at the point of entry.

Has there been a slackening of the vowels since Labor came into power? Or have we as a nation always spoken in true Aussie terms.

—Tony Murphy, *Sunday Times*

This isn't great journalism or original political linguistic theory, but the ideas and attitudes are representative enough and make this a useful text on which to begin a reading of the Australian accent. Murphy's tone masks an ambivalent attitude towards the phenomenon he is describing. He pretends to be celebrating a new millennium, joining in the new language and the new freedom:

'Now we'll all talk in real Aussie lingo'. But as he sees it, that freedom to be at last really Australian is essentially the loss of standards. The core meaning of the accent for him is the 'slackness' of its vowels, symbol of a creeping slackness in political and social life. This slackness has affiliations with both ideology (Labor) and class (hostility to those who are privately educated, a traditional governing class).

To Murphy the accent has strong claims to being the real Australian language, yet he also tries to believe that before Hawke's election victory the Australian language was different; that 'the Australian language' then was the kind of language spoken by Liberal prime ministers and other members of their class. He speculates on two causal explanations. Perhaps Hawke's influence and Labor's victory has created a vowel shift and attitude shift, or at least legitimated it. Or perhaps that shift in values as expressed through accent had already occurred, discrediting Liberal politicians and ensuring a Hawke victory. Either way Murphy is using accents as materials for the construction of a contemporary myth of the Fall. In this Fall, the triumph of Labor (or the demise of the Liberals as the natural party of government) marks the victory of Australian nationalism at the expense of the possibility of Australian achievement. For Murphy, the Australian accent signifies absolute hostility to excellence.

The politics of Murphy's theory of accents are clear enough, but that isn't to say that Hawkespeak doesn't exist as a significant political phenomenon. Hawkespeak is a crucial component of the Hawke image, the Hawke myth, which as we write this in early 1986 still gains a 67 per cent approval rating in opinion polls. That makes it no mean political weapon. Part of Hawkespeak is found in Hawke's vowels, as he says classic phrases like 'Ahh, goodday!', the voice harsh and strong, the open vowel of 'ah' coming through a strangulated throat and letterbox mouth. This is easily identifiable as broad Australian, the quintessential language of Australian mateship. But there is another aspect of Hawkespeak which Murphy satirises through the phrase 'in respect of'. Max Gillies' brilliant parody of Hawke strings together innumerable vacuous circumlocutions like this around a minuscule content. This isn't the working-class language of mateship. On the contrary, it's a middle-class elaborate form of speech which constitutes the traditional language of politics, as Australians see it. But Hawke speaks this language with a curious combination of incompetence and excess, as though it's a dialect he hasn't quite learnt. It is analogous to the clothes he wears and the way he wears them: pinstripe suits which look as though they don't quite belong, cuff links he fiddles with obsessively as if wishing he or they weren't there.

But Hawke isn't a populist prime minister because he finds it difficult to speak educated English. Also central to the Hawke myth is his status as a Rhodes scholar, a graduate of Oxford University. You can't get much further 'out of the country' than that, or deeper into the heartland of the elite. Yet while he was there he broke a world record for drinking beer, thus subverting the traditions of Oxford University and Rhodes scholarships, and retaining links with his Oz cultural roots. Nonetheless, he was there, where Malcolm Fraser had been with somewhat less academic distinction. The myth is a kind of proof of Hawke's status as a mediator of contradictions, which is one of the typical functions of mythic heroes.

So Hawkespeak and the Hawke myth are built on a contradiction. Far from detracting from his appeal, the contradictions are essential to it. The accent and manner are so powerful a creator of authenticity and solidarity for many ordinary Australians that they seem not to notice that what he says in this accent jettisons large sections of the Labor platform. For others, it is this policy content which makes Hawke seem 'the best Liberal prime minister since Menzies'. But it would be implausible to suggest that so many people are failing to see through such an obvious contradiction. There are plenty of politicians on right and left who offer the alternatives in a purer form, and none are challengers to Hawke. It's the contradictions, seemingly yoked together in a single person, that the voters want, an Australia which is both a contradiction and a unity.

This problem and this solution weren't invented by Labor or Hawke. Peacock's accent is an Australian one, and in fact he won a televised debate against Hawke before the 1984 elections by being more of a larrikin than Hawke, on that occasion. Peacock's successor as Liberal leader, John Howard, suffers from an image problem whose core is its narrowness of appeal. In the Liberal ranks there are speakers of broad Australian, who are indispensible to the party's tactics and image: people such as Wilson Tuckey and Bruce Goodluck, with a debating style that matches their vowels. Far from alienating Liberal voters, this accent and style reassures many, so long as it coexists with its opposite. The Liberal party, too, aspires after potent contradictions, not an impotent purity.

Even the hero of Liberal myth, Bob Menzies, represented a 1950s form of the same contradiction: an unashamed royalist and Anglophile who helped to dismantle the British connection, whose famous 'wit' consisted mainly of crude jibes against hecklers, his vowels flattened into typical Australian forms by a typical letterbox mouth. Even his nickname, Pig Iron Bob, was a gift from his enemies which he turned to good use. Coined as a reminder of a trade deal with the Japanese before the Second World War, a deal that cast doubt on his patriotism, it became detached from that meaning. Instead it sounded like a working-class tribute, in authentic working-class language. Thus the Australian language unwittingly helped to sustain his legitimacy as an ordinary Australian, while his credentials as a member of the ruling elite remained unquestioned.

Murphy's ambivalence towards 'Aussie lingo' and the Hawke phenomenon points to important fissures in Australian social and political life. The Australian accent is uncontested as the dominant definition of Australianness, yet it is skewed towards working-class Australian values and ideology. Of course, not all Australian citizens are working class or want to affirm these values and speak this accent. For this kind of Australian the Australian accent is attractive, because it is the symbol of identity, but it is also the marker of a class and lifestyle they see as beneath them. The conflict threatens their sense of themselves as truly Australian. In Australia, successful politicians must to some extent satisfy two groups and two ideologies. One is an ideology of excellence as defined by the ruling elite, with their conviction that only under their management can Australia achieve it. The other is the ideology of Australianness as carried by the Australian accent. There's no simple formula for achieving a successful mix or balance. It is in the context of this kind of struggle that the Australian accent has acquired its ambiguous status and strategic importance, the one depending on the other.

Flat brown speech: The meaning of the Australian accent

I believe that the colonial accent in Australia is due to the effects of an inflammation of the nose, a complaint from which most Australians seem to suffer. The prevalent nose inflammation is probably due to pollen in the air, there are thousands of grasses in Australia which produce this pollen.

—Dr Halliday Sutherland, *Daily Telegraph*, 28 March 1940

Dr Sutherland's breakthrough in explaining the Australian accent has sadly lacked disciples. Among scholars there is a large measure of agreement about what constitutes the Australian accent and who speaks it, but its origins and causes are shrouded in mystery. Some things are clear. Its basis seems to have been some kind of mix of working-class urban English dialects. But it's not just a mixture, a little bit of Cockney plus bits of other dialects. It's a single accent, marked by a systemic shift that has affected a whole class of sounds of the language in the same direction. This distinctive shift seems to have happened remarkably early in the history of the colony and to have been inexplicably comprehensive. If there are regional variations of the Australian accent, as some claim, they are minute compared to the overall consistency of the accent across Australia, in regional centres separated sometimes by thousands of inhospitable miles. This whole revolution in language had essentially occurred by the 1830s, unassisted and barely noticed by the ruling elite. By 1880 it had essentially the same distinctive forms as today.

It is worth while to consider some implications of this history. In the nineteenth-century movement towards the creation of Australia as a political entity, which culminated in Federation in 1901, the leading figures recorded by history are mainly from the middle classes. But a British-educated ruling class did not invent a different language or a different culture. While they were deploring the colonial lack of standards, in language as in culture, and long before they as a group had conceived of the idea of a new national identity, the blueprint for the new national language and culture had been laid down, inscribed in an accent and a set of values. In practice, this constituted a coherent and systematic assault on some of the defining features of British English. Without it, the new Australia of the founding fathers would have been only a new political arrangement, not a new nation. The enabling conditions came from below, a radical creative act on a scale which the modern middle-class Australian is still reluctant to acknowledge or accept. Nor was this a once-for-all act of creation and appropriation. The pattern is alive and well today, as we saw with the language of politics. Even in Australia today, creativity still comes from below and is appropriated from above. Change that is recognised as both real and Australian, still, will have popular or working-class markers attached. Hence the phenomenon of middle-class obsession with ockerism, a symbolic attempt to both incorporate and control it.

Academic linguists following the pioneering work of Professor A.G. Mitchell pretty much agree on the main features of the accent, but their books are difficult for non-specialists, because of the need for technical phonetic description. Fortunately Australia has an alternative school of linguistic theory whose main findings are compatible with those of the academic theorists and much easier to understand. These are the satirists and parodists of the Australian language, people such as Nino Culotta (J. O'Grady) and Afferbeck Lauder (A. Morrison) in the 1960s and Barry Humphreys, Paul Hogan and the *Australia You're Standing in It* team of the 1980s. Here is a contribution to Australian linguistics from *Australia You're Standing in It* (hereafter *AYSI*):

Neville Shoot's
A Brown like Bryan
Scene: Malaya 1942

[*Camera tracks through junglegrowth to two figures sitting on a bench,* HELEN *dressed in Edwardian dress, buttoned up to the neck,* BRYAN *in singlet and shorts*]

HELEN [*voice quavering with emotion*]: The Japanese are so crewel!

BRYAN [*pulls large nail out of his hand with a hammer with no observable expression*]: Moy word.

[*Pause*]

HELEN: And this jungle—it's so hostile! The colours are so different from the soft pastel watercolour hues of my home in England.

[*Pause*]

BRYAN: What part?

HELEN [*head shaking from side to side with intensity*]: Have you heard . . . of the Lakelands?

BRYAN: Moy word. Thet's whether carlid pairncils carmfrum.

[*Pause*]

HELEN: What is it like where *you* come from?

BRYAN: Flet. Flet unbraown. It's braown in winter. An spring. It's vairy braown in spring. Moy word?

HELEN: And in summer?

BRYAN: Sarmmer. In sarmmer the big braown carms daown frum the north, an it gets real braown. Braown as a byeby's barm.

In this sketch, *AYSI* have exaggerated the key features of Australian English, and linked them maliciously to certain qualities of character. But better a malicious interpretation than none at all. Bryan's language contrasts with Helen's in a number of ways which help to define the accent as a whole. Apart from the distinctive vowels, she articulates very precisely, missing no consonants, giving a purer value to almost every vowel (though 'crewel' gets a little extra work done on it). Bryan drops consonants and slides words together (e.g. 'whether' for 'where the'). Her intonation is richly varied, with expressive highs and lows. His is typical Australian: flat and brown, with less high and low, less difference between emphatic and non-emphatic words. But there is one distinctive Australian feature in his intonation. His voice often rises at the end of sentences, as though they were questions or he sought some form of reassurance. Even his oath, 'moy word', sounds like a question more than an exclamation. In general Helen turns statements into exclamations where he turns them into questions.

But the focus of the accent is the vowels. Six of these are particularly important in the Australian accent, the vowels in the words 'my', 'flat', 'brown', 'come' 'very' and 'baby'. All of Bryan's vowels are different from those in 'standard English', but in these instances his have crossed over into the territory occupied by other vowels. We've tried to use normal English spelling as a device to foreground these shifts, but not of course to render them precisely. In any case, it's not important to catch these as isolated sounds, so much as the underlying quality the shifts have in common.

Vowels and consonants have distinct properties and hence meanings. Vowels come from the lungs and the larynx, as sound and energy from within, easy and natural. Consonants interrupt this flow of sound, breaking it up, requiring effort, precision and control of the vocal apparatus. So consonants tend to signify culture, constraint and control; and vowels tend to signify the opposite—nature, emotion, freedom. 'Correct' speech in all varieties of English prides itself on getting consonants right. Dropping consonants is a general signifier of relaxed, informal, intimate speech. So the Australian tendency to drop consonants is part of a widespread phenomenon and is easily understood by speakers of English. By some criteria it shows 'slackness' or 'laziness'. By other criteria it is 'relaxed', 'natural', 'informal'. It's only a fault of speech and character if everyone is expected to be tight, formal and full of effort all the time.

But Australian vowels aren't exactly slack. A major underlying feature of its vowel system is a tendency towards 'closure'. This involves some movement towards closure of the oral cavity and some movement of the point of articulation of the sound towards the front of the mouth (plus a bit of the nasalisation that excited Dr Sutherland). The most potent factor in the Australian accent is the Australian letterbox mouth, of which Hawke has a fine example. It has been said that the way to sound Australian is never to move the upper lip. It has also been claimed that Australian speech has been determined by the danger of flies entering an open mouth. The Australian accent is English as spoken through the Australian mouth. Or from another point of view, the Australian mouth is the stamp of the Australian accent on the Australian face. But is it mere laziness, a refusal to move lips and jaw any more than necessary, as popular critics have so often claimed? It may be something more purposive and definite, a specific act of constraint. The lips don't get out of the way to allow the mouth cavity to enhance resonance. On the contrary, the mouth acts to damp down the sound, and the corners of the mouth press downwards. The Australian accent is minimalistic and reductive, but it requires its own kind of effort, too. It isn't simply laziness. If it was, it would sound like English spoken lazily, which it doesn't.

By the way they have dramatised this exchange, *AYSI* imply a social reading of this accent. Bryan's accent signifies self-control, self-repression, even the death of feeling (he shows no sign of pain when pulling the nail out, and no response to Helen's warmth and beauty). In contrast, Helen's accent represents a combination of expressiveness with precision and control. Behind this we can see a stereotypical judgment on Australians (especially males) as incapable of finer feelings, unable to express intimacy or to relate to those of the other sex. But this is not quite the meaning inscribed into the two accents. Helen's precision is a conformity to innumerable external constraints. The emotional range, conveyed through pitch variation and an expressive vocabulary, inevitably seems a contrived overcompensation. Bryan's accent is an inner-directed and wholistic holding back, not an externally oriented conformity to detailed prescriptions. If his accent signifies a wariness or distrust of closeness, her accent signifies spurious emotionality which he would do well to be suspicious of. But the upwards lift at the end of his sentences acts as a polite invitation to solidarity. It's not a question, but like questions it encourages a response, seeming to include the other in the discourse.

Two aspects of what he says deserve further comment. One is

his expletive. He has only one, 'my word', which he overuses. As we know, the stereotypical Australian vocabulary has three words which are much more common and equally overused: 'bloody', 'shit', and 'fuck' (and derivatives). 'Bloody' was at one time called the Great Australian Adjective, even though it was not an Australian coinage. Nor are the other two. But absolute novelty is not the point with an accent. Rather, an accent is derived from specific patternings. The pattern with these expletives is as follows. First take a common taboo word for a taboo object or process (sexual or excremental). Then partly empty it of its referential meaning, focusing instead on its taboo status. Finally use the word so commonly and frequently that the taboo loses its force. The result is a word with an infinitely expandable range of uses, all of which can be guaranteed to make well-bred speakers of English feel vaguely uncomfortable.

As with other aspects of the Australian language, this linguistic creativity starts from a process of radical stripping, exercised against the English language itself. This negativity is what typically strikes middle-class commentators. They see it as a sign of the emotional and mental impoverishment of Australians. They hear words that are familiar but forbidden to them, and they presume that vulgar Australians simply lack the culture that should repress these words. They hear the same word being repeated and see it as a mindless repetition, failing to see that the use of the same word in a large number of contexts can give it an almost unmanageable complexity of meanings and functions.

In fact the Australian use of expletives does not ignore taboos; it defies them. Taboos against their use remain in force in Australia, inscribed in statute books. In 1985 the Western Australian police charged the Sydney comedian Rodney Rude with obscenity for using one of the Big Three to excess in his stage show. They counted 30 uses of this word in a 90-minute show, deducing with impeccable mathematics that the word was used on average once every 3 minutes. It is true that there would probably have been no prosection for this offence in most other states of Australia, and even in Western Australia the decision was overturned by the Full Court, in April 1986. They ruled that context was crucial, according to the newspaper report.

> Used in combination with the word 'off', the offending word was vulgar and quite impolite, but well understood and not necessarily obscene. The word's primary meaning was 'to copulate' but

more often than not it was used simply as a strong expletive, and repeated use had tended to lessen the impact.

—*West Australian*, 22 April 1986

These enlightened views about the Australian language now have the force of law. But the court was not opening the floodgates to Australian slang. The Chief Justice is reported to have insisted that 'the use of a single taboo word could amount to disorderly conduct'. (Another W.A. comedian, Kevin 'Bloody' Wilson, takes no risks in his use of the word; he claims to pronounce it with a 'ph...'.) There are public places and public places, and had Rodney Rude said the word in Hay Street Mall he would have been guilty of obscenity and disorderly conduct. The court, then, was not declaring this word non-taboo. All that was at issue was a small and hard-won shift in the places where it could be used. The right of the State remained intact: it could police the Australian language and keep offending portions of it out of public Australian spaces.

A characteristically Australian form of creativity can be seen in Bryan's use of the single word 'brown'. As with the use of expletives, repetition of a single word can be taken as a sign of an impoverished vocabulary and an impoverished mind. In contrast Helen's language (e.g. 'soft pastel watercolour hues') seems a precise and subtle instrument for recording a range of precisely discriminated shades—a superior, more refined sensibility. But Helen's language shows an undistinguished and unoriginal elaboration of terms. Bryan's reduction of the world of colours to the single brown is itself a creative step, giving the word a new plenitude of meanings and associations. The typical Australian form created by adding 'the' creates a new concept out of these simple building blocks: 'the big brown'. In Bryan's mouth it's a joke, of course, but it still has an effect akin to poetry, an effect that is quintessentially Australian.

In correcting some common negative judgments on the Australian accent we don't want to go to the other extreme. The virtues of Australian English as we have described them are not unique. On the contrary they have a family resemblance to many other forms of working-class language. That is one of the reasons why the ocker is so recognisable and significant a phenomenon overseas. Nor do we suggest that these qualities are always strengths, in all circumstances. But to see the accent as an inadvertent failure to appreciate the virtue of 'proper English' is clearly wrong. The Australian accent contains its own distinctive ideology, its own prescriptions about how human relationships should be conducted. That ideology has its own problems and contradictions. It repudiates external constraints, yet develops its own forms of self-repression. It is egalitarian and oriented towards social solidarity, yet it establishes clear boundaries and ample spaces around individuals, allowing them to be both vulnerable and defensive. In a pure form this ideology and its accompanying form of language are not suited to conditions of either great intimacy or elaborate public display. But then, accents are never monolithic and rigid forms, prisons of language and thought. Every Australian can move in and out of the Australian accent as occasion demands. The creation of the Australian accent remains a significant cultural achievement, of which Australians do well to feel proud, in spite of so much prestigious criticism of it.

Cricket, thongs and Vegemite: An Australian cultural accent

An accent is not just a collection of isolated and meaningless features of sound. Rather, it is a systemic and meaningful shift. This shift affects a whole range of elements of the language in similar ways to express a common complex set of social meanings. Exactly the same phenomenon occurs in the same way for the same reasons outside verbal language. There is an Australian 'accent', a distinctive way of doing many other things which creates a national identity in the same way as speech forms do. It is recognisably the same identity, although as we look at these other forms we also get a due sense of the diversity of that identity.

For purposes of illustration we will look at three examples of an Australian cultural accent. We begin with an older instance, the example of Vegemite. For about 40 years the place of Vegemite in Australian mythology was assured. It was almost a national addiction for Australians, to the bewilderment of outsiders, who failed to see the obsessive appeal of the sticky black substance. Yet Michael Symons in his persuasive critique of Australian cuisine, *One Continuous Picnic*, is scathing of Vegemite. He points out that it was an adaptation of the English Marmite, and hence unoriginal; made from brewer's yeast, ironic in the light of its claims to be a health food; and American owned, from 1936 onwards, when Kraft took over the company founded by Fred Walker.

All of these criticisms have some truth. But the fact that it's a creative adaptation of brewer's waste doesn't in the least challenge its Australianness. On the contrary this is a typical feature of the Australian accent. As a food its characteristic is no-nonsense flexibility. Like Bryan's use of 'brown', it's a portable, concentrated, multipurpose commodity. Modern dieticians criticise its salt content, especially now that fast foods contain so much added salt, but in the 1930s the fast food phenomenon was a long way off. And the vitamins it contained, before science had quite determined what they were or what they did, are indeed extremely valuable items in a healthy diet. It is hard to see what more Symons could have asked of this humble foodstuff, except perhaps that it be less humble.

His final point, however, deserves further comment. It is true that American interests own the company that produces Vegemite. Symons' book points out many other examples of this paradox. It is in fact a widespread phenomenon in Australian culture for outside interests to control and exploit markers of Australianness. It makes Australian culture seem inauthentic, merely a branch of American or British capitalism. And as we saw, the Australian accent itself is constantly being appropriated and exploited by an entrepreneurial class, parasitically mocking it for pleasure and profit. We shouldn't ignore these hostile forces, nor should we attribute an easy or inevitable success to them. Cultural genocide would be too easy if ownership of a commodity was enough to achieve it. Australians shouldn't be complacent about rip-offs of their culture by foreign or local capitalists, but nor should they repudiate a genuine Australian cultural achievement as soon as the rip-off happens. Cultures that come from below are conditioned to expect exploitation from above, and they display their own strategies of survival and resistance.

Another example of the Australian accent we will take is the ubiquitous thong. ('How can you tell Australians abroad? By the gap between their big toes and the rest.') The thong is the contemporary Australian accent of footwear. As it flops over our sidewalks and beaches it speaks of our warm climate whose scorching pavements and sand demand the minimal veneer of culture to protect our (white) feet from the harsh excesses of nature. It speaks of our informality, of our easy acceptance of our bodies, of our wish to bring the outdoors indoors. Its cheapness bears our egalitarianism. It is the distinctive Australian footwear, and shaping it like the country, as illustrated here, merely exaggerates what is already there. The fact that the rubber and the idea probably come from

The all-Australian thong

Asia doesn't make it any the less part of an Australian accent, any more than Australian speech needed to reinvent the alphabet. Patterns of use are what makes an accent, and Asians are well aware that the Australian use of the thongs makes them a different species of footwear.

But like Australian expletives, it is kept safely on one side of the class divide. Predictably the thong is banned from the hallowed floors of classy bars and restaurants. Here the constraint of shoes is the only acceptable accent; 'true' Australianness is banished in the interests of smartness. The thong is as loose and sloppy as the ocker accent; shoes are as tight and polished as the respectable voice with its echoes of Europe. Most of us switch readily from thongs to shoes and from a broader to a more polished accent as the social situation requires. In the accent of footwear as of voice, raising the class decreases the Australianness.

No account of the Australian cultural accent is complete without mention of sport. Here, as with other instances we have looked at, we have the puzzling phenomenon of something distinctively Australian whose uniqueness is hard to demonstrate. The Australian approach to sport strikes the visitor as characteristic, yet we didn't invent most of these sports nor our enthusiasm for them. How could this be part of the Australian national character? But then, how could it be ignored? Here the concept of accent is useful, since it deals with significant shifts and patterns of shift, not with absolute differences. And the meanings of sport, like other aspects of accent, manifestly serve to define Australianness, and they're used by the same kind of person to denigrate Australianness for the same reasons.

Australian Rules Football is the easiest example to analyse, because it is sufficiently unique and proclaims itself the national game of football. It isn't unique, of course. Like any accent it readapts existing forms and codes. Essentially it takes a Rugby ball and modified Rugby roles, on a cricket oval, incorporating some reminiscences of Gaelic football. Like any accent there are many particular differences, but these differences form a pattern which makes the same kind of sense, with the same kind of social meaning. We can summarise some of the differences from Rugby as follows:

Rugby	**Australian Rules**
1. *Interrupted flow*	*Free flow*
No forward passing	Free passing
Throwing ball	Punching ball
Movement along ground	Movement through air
Strong tackling	Constrained tackling
Running with ball	Kicking ball
Articulated space	Free space
2. *Complex scoring*	*Cumulative scoring*
Different modes:	Same mode:
try plus goal	6 + 1 points
Precise target	Reward for near miss
Lower totals	Higher totals

These differences are not absolute, they are only shifts of emphasis. But the shifts are in the same direction, towards less constraint, less precision, towards unimpeded flow, although one with its own constraints built in. There is still physical contact, but there is greater space and greater freedom of movement. There are more players to a team, in a looser form of organisation. It is unequivocally a team sport, not an individual one, but individual autonomy is continuous, not isolated in spectacular moments as with the Rugby try. The conscious reason for some of these differences was the different physical playing conditions in Australia, just as the spoken accent is sometimes attributed to Australia's wide open spaces, but the social meanings they share undoubtedly had their own crucial role to play.

Cricket seems a more difficult sport in terms of which to show the presence of an Australian accent, since Australians ostensibly play by the same rules as every other nation. But ways of playing cricket are used to construct an Australian identity, and this is used as part of the same ideological game as is deployed on ways of speaking. As one instance, we will take the phenomenon of one-day cricket. This game is a specific accent of the game of cricket, and it is contrasted to Test cricket in the same way as lower-class accents are to 'standard' English. Here is an upper-class English commentator, Henry Blofeld, reflecting on the game in the *Australian* newspaper, 18 February 1984.

> Constant short pitched bowling in one-day cricket, the emphasis on pace at the expense of spin, and also the covering of pitches here all had an effect.
>
> But then, the colossal crowds which have turned up to watch probably the worst of the five Benson & Hedges World Series Cup competitions—there were only two tight finishes—reflect a social need.
>
> Crowds these days are hooked on the drug of sensation. They are not worried if the quality falls off as long as they get their kick. Of course, the one-day international cricket is a gold mine, and in Australia it has gained an unstoppable momentum of its own.

From this we can reconstruct what Blofeld sees as the crucial shifts from traditional cricket that make up this new accent in cricket. The length of the game is the crucial feature—one day as against five days for Tests, which often don't finish even then. Like Australian Rules, the one-day game maximises difference to produce a result. It has 'sensation' which Blofeld dismisses with contempt. It offers 'tight finishes' (though not always, as he points out acerbically) as against the 'loose finishes' (tame predictable draws, presumably) of Test cricket. But it is the social differences which for Blofeld are the clearest proof of a loss of standards—for similar reasons to Murphy, discussed at the beginning of this chapter. The crime of one-day cricket is that it is commercially successful ('a gold mine') and popular ('colossal crowds'). For someone like

Blofeld the causal link between popularity and decline of standards is absolute, just as elitism is sufficient proof of excellence.

In the recent development of the one-day game, media coverage has played an important role. One-day cricket in Australia in many respects is constructed as a media event, with many of its features adapted to television coverage. Paradoxically, in spite of one-day cricket attracting much larger crowds than Test cricket, these crowds seem to exist for the sake of the even larger TV audience. The live crowd thus is part of the show, communicating with the mass audience (or itself as included in that larger audience) via placards that can be read on the screen as TV cameras obligingly zoom in. During the play itself, a barrage of statistics and replays from different angles keeps spectators continually informed.

The tendency in all this is towards increased activity, an enhanced role for the crowd. Though a Blofeld could regret the populism inherent in it, others could note the success with which the Packer organisation has turned this into a profitable commodity. In contrast, Test cricket has been designed more for an elite, and is controlled by that elite. Until recently media coverage was in the hands of the ABC, the 'national' station, as part of its function of creating an appropriate image for the nation. The essence of the ABC style or accent is reticence: camera work and commentary understate and underplay the action and its effects. A Blofeld is reassured by this restrained style, whose qualities match exactly the qualities of the elite form of the game he also prefers. Commercial coverage and the one-day game share crudity with the great Australian adjective.

The connection of the one-day accent with Australia is oblique, in Blofeld's text. Australia didn't invent the one-day game (in fact village cricket, ancestor of traditional cricket, preceded it by hundreds of years as a one-day form). West Indies are the current champions. Yet the popularity of the game in Australia, together with the role of Kerry Packer in marketing it, make it seem a distinctively Australian form, a part of contemporary Australian culture in spite of its international status.

Blofeld is also hostile to fast bowling, seeing this as part of a new accent in the game that he doesn't like. Again, Australians didn't invent fast bowling (and Blofeld is even more critical of West Indians, who are also too fond of it). But it's an attitude to fast bowling that he condemns, especially as exemplified by Dennis Lillee. Lillee has this symbolic, even mythic, meaning for Australians as well. The difference is that Australians admire what Blofeld deplores. As a bowler, Lillee has an aggressive, win-at-all-costs attitude which comes out as an apparent wish not simply to dismiss English batsmen but to terrify them as well. In the shift from batting to bowling, and within bowling from the guile of spin to the raw directness of pace, Blofeld detects the same meaning: a frank declaration of the aggression and hostility that in the traditional game is masked by the elegance of the master batsman (a 'responsible' craftsman, not a crude slogger) and the intricate precision of the spinner.

Dennis Lillee has other qualities that have assured him a place in Australian mythology. Not only does he demonstrate frank hostility towards opponents, but he has a less than fully respectful attitude towards authority, as represented by umpires and by wimpish Establishment-supported captains. And he lacks an inbred decorum that clearly has a class dimension, which comes out in what Blofeld calls Lillee's 'antics'. Blofeld never specifically mentions the class that Lillee represents, but this is at the core of what Lillee means for both Blofeld and the Australian crowds. This meaning is given new potency by being allied to the meanings of fast bowling. A great fast bowler of a century ago, Spofforth, was immediately nicknamed 'The Demon', and fast bowlers are commonly termed 'demon bowlers'. Cricket as a game has long roots, going back to rituals that referred to chthonic forces, destructive and creative, that had to be celebrated and tamed. There is a latent structure of meanings in the game, far older than Australian culture, waiting for a Dennis Lillee to fill his foreordained place in it. He becomes a symbol of the forces from below of 'nature', which priests of the threatened 'higher culture' like Blofeld will attempt to denigrate and exorcise if they cannot control them.

Work as accent: The myth of the Lucky Country

The importance of the Australian accent is not confined to the fields of sport, leisure and entertainment. Just as Australianness is a vital ingredient in any successful political campaign, so it is also an integral part of ideological strategies designed to sell particular analyses of the 'Australian problem'. At the core of this strategy is an attempt to lay the blame for Australia's economic problems on the ingrained habits of the Australian worker. A talismanic phrase often invoked is 'the Lucky Country', coined by Donald Horne in the 1960s. This projects a myth that sets the material wealth of Australia against a complacent and feckless populace squandering its inheritance. The typical Australian at the centre of this myth is easily recognisable as the slack speaker of slack vowels that we have already seen.

To show a contemporary use of this myth we will draw on an article published in the *Australian* on 26 April 1986. Its title proclaimed: 'The demise of the Lucky Country. Now it's a challenge for excellence.' Under a photo of Senator Button it summarised his position as follows: 'Senator Button—has diagnosed that our trading crisis is cultural in its essence and requires a pervasive cure'. That is, Australia's problem is the Australian character as inscribed in Australian culture, and its defining feature is its repudiation of excellence. The solution becomes equally obvious though drastic: an attack on that culture itself, preserving the nation at the cost of the culture.

But in the article Senator Button, a Labor Cabinet minister, doesn't quite say that. The myth is powerful enough for headline-writing, but not the whole of Button's speech. He does criticise trade unions, especially for what he sees as unnecessary strikes. But he also praises their capacity to respond to technological innovation: 'Trade unions have come an enormous way in terms of understanding the terms of trade issue, an enormous way', he says. 'They have come far more than the rest of the community in three years.' In the same article another Labor minister, John Dawkins, gives his own analysis: 'Once again, as a nation, we are in danger of being an also-ran. Among the last to relinquish the past and embrace the future. Our own conservatism, our own anglophilia, our cultural myopia, indeed our racism, could again be our undoing.' Some of these criticisms fit the stereotype Australian of the Lucky Country, but not all do—certainly not conservatism and Anglophilia. And Dawkins in fact was addressing a business group, not workers, seeing this as a problem of management not labour.

In fact the Australian accent and the values inscribed in it might have much to offer an Australian economic renaissance. The Australian character might be our greatest resource, not our major problem. To see some of its more positive aspects we will take the following pair of photographs as a text. These appeared on the front page of the *Wanneroo Times*, a local Western Australian newspaper, on Tuesday 5 March 1985. One shows Don Kaptain,

THE DOCTOR DOES HIS ROUNDS

... and finds the going tough

Wanneroo Councillor Dr Wayne Bradshaw swapped the air-conditioned comfort of his surgery last week for a stint on the road with the shire's garbos.

And although Dr Bradshaw says he saw a full day out on the shire's collection unit 51, he was spending more time in the cab of the truck than out by the end of the day.

Apart from a sunburnt lip and a couple of blisters Dr Bradshaw says he also came away with a healthy respect for the work that the garbos do.

Cr Bradshaw joined the round last Wednesday to get some first hand information on the troubles which are currently plaguing the shire's collection service.

"We've had the best rubbish collection service in the State for many years," Cr Bradshaw said.

Rubbish collections in some suburbs of the shire have been up to a day late over the past two weeks.

Cr Bradshaw says the troubles are a combination of the heat, which naturally enough slowed the men down, the trucks overheating and a new police directive which stops collectors riding on the backs of trucks.

"The new police stand that collectors cannot ride on the backs of trucks means that each collector now has to walk about an extra 15 kilometres a day," he said.

"Some of the rounds are still up to a day behind, but we've brought in some additional units and we hope to clear the backlog up shortly," he said.

"Personally I think the new police directive is unnecessary, as the collectors are fairly safety conscious, and are not going to ride down Marmion Avenue or Whitford Avenue on the back of a truck.

"They are only riding from one house to the next, and a truck certainly can't gather much speed in that distance."

● A rubbish bin sits easily on the shoulders of Don Kaptain, of Wanneroo who's been collecting rubbish with the Wanneroo Shire for more than 14 years....

... but a full bin of rubbish doesn't rest quite so easily on the shoulders of Wanneroo Councillor, Dr Wayne Bradshaw.

The accent of Dr Garbo

unequivocally working class, a shire garbo for fourteen years. The other shows Dr Wayne Bradshaw, Deputy Shire President of Wanneroo Shire Council, a large shire to the north of Perth, someone at the other end of the social scale. The conjunction of the two makes an obvious ideological point: this is an image of harmony of worker and boss. But it's worth looking closely at the terms of this reconciliation and the crucial role that is played by different accents in this ideological construction.

Both men are dressed in clothes that are typical of working-class Australian men. The clothes they have in common are shorts, a cap and a red jacket over a casual form of shirt. Dr Wayne's gleaming new boots are visible in the photo: Don Kaptain almost certainly has boots on as well, though probably less gleaming and new. The cap and red jacket are not typically Australian, but their clothing below the waist is. Archetypal Australians, like Paul Hogan as Hoges and Harry Butler as Harry Butler, wear a similar uniform. The shorts are an adaptation to the hot Australian climate. They also signify casualness, simplicity and lack of constraint, just as the speech accent does: legs bare to the sun, unencumbered by clothing and the demands of culture. The dark blue colour is functional in not showing the dirt, not requiring frequent washing, merging with the dust and dirt of a workplace, not trying to resist it or impose standards of cleanliness on it. The boots, however, carry a different meaning. They are thick boots, offering heavy protection at the price of freedom of movement. If the shorts represent a kind of freedom and a confident oneness with the environment, the boots represent the opposite, a suspicion of the dangers of the workplace. They carry the opposite meaning to thongs, yet are equally Australian. Accents don't have to be consistent.

But if garbos' clothes are a kind of accent, a significant selection from and displacement of the general clothing code, Dr Wayne's clothes are an inflection of this accent. Where Don Kaptain's shorts are dark blue and creased with wear, Dr Wayne's are light blue, neatly tailored and still well pressed. Don Kaptain's shirt is open halfway down his chest, and his red jacket is unbuttoned. Dr Wayne wears a white T-shirt, with his loyalty to the Wanneroo Shire inscribed on the front. This clothing is both casual and yet circumspect, more appropriate to a doctor relaxing in his back garden than to a garbo or any other 'blue-collar' worker. In these ways Dr Wayne gives an upper-class twist to the working-class clothes he has put on. By these displacements he signifies precision, constraint and correctness, even when he is consciously trying to relax and project the opposite meaning. He is sending a double message: as one of the workers, yet still an influential and important person, a doctor and a shire councillor.

But it's not entirely easy for an Australian boss like Dr Bradshaw to signify working-class qualities. The photographs suggest a marked contrast in how they do this job. Don Kaptain is strongly built and holds the rubbish bin with a superbly economical stance, with his arm straight so that the weight bears down through his shoulder, putting minimal strain on his biceps or triceps. Dr Bradshaw as a doctor could probably explain the physiology involved, but as a garbo for a day he hasn't quite been able to resolve the practical problems. His body is twisted awkwardly, and the bottom of the bin digs (probably painfully) into his shoulder, his left arm is bent to take the weight, but his body weight rests on his right leg, putting further torsion on his spine. His watch is probably digging uncomfortably into his wrist. The baroque elaborations of his stance contrast with the bare economy and efficiency, honed down by many years of practice, of Don Kaptain's way of handling bins.

It's unsurprising, of course, that Don Kaptain is better with bins than Dr Bradshaw. And if we put an anaesthetised patient in front of them, and a scalpel in their hand, no doubt Bradshaw would have a better operating technique. However, there's one difference between the skills. Society recognises and values the skill of a surgeon highly, but it doesn't even acknowledge that there could be a skill in what is labelled 'unskilled work'. We don't need to claim any equality of value, however that might be assessed, to see the basic asymmetry of judgment. Skill and culture are definitionally what doctors have and garbos don't. Bradshaw, after a day's experience, acknowledges a new respect for garbos, but the details mentioned are his sunburnt lips and blisters, as though garbos have rougher skin but that's all.

A way of handling rubbish bins is an 'accent' just as much as ways of dressing and speaking, and we can read it by the same principles. And the invisible messages of Don Kaptain's technique carry meanings similar to some of those we have seen in speech and clothes: a spare simplicity, a paring down of irrelevant excrescences, whether actions or consonants or syllables and words. This quality is not uniquely Australian—much of the Australian accent has affinities with other lower-class, regional accents, and the affinities are no accident. What is important to insist on, though, is that Don Kaptain's skill, although a minor achievement in itself and deployed on a humble task, is not inherently ridiculous, any more than the Australian accent is inherently ridiculous, in spite of the impression given by a hundred years of middle-class satire. This facility for stripping off excrescences isn't purely negative or destructive. On the contrary, it's the precondition for a kind of creativity. It wasn't upper-class speakers who invented a new distinctive Australian accent or evolved new clothing styles. The Australian accent signifies creativity coming from below. Senator Button and John Dawkins could do well to take note, in their role as diagnosticians of Australian culture.

The particular kind of inventiveness that we argue is implicit in the Australian accent can be seen as widespread in Australian life. In 1984, for instance, 15 936 patents were applied for by Australians, the second highest rate per capita in the world. Inventions can be complicated constructs, Heath Robinson machines with hundreds of different parts, but the typical Australian invention is simple in conception, practical, reduced to essentials. The boomerang—invented by Aborigines long before whites came to Australia—is a classic Australian invention, achieving its effects by subtle changes of shape and by techniques of throwing. In 1982, Eric Willmott, an Aborigine, was named inventor of the year for his new system of gearing, a radical simplification of existing systems. Ralph Sarich's orbital engine similarly is smaller, lighter, with fewer moving parts, and better fuel economy than existing engines. The success of the *Australia II* yacht was due in no small degree to Ben Lexcen's invention of the 'winged keel'. Or we could go further back in time, to new pieces of equipment, invented by farmers to solve practical problems: Ridley's stripper, the rotary hoe, Smith's stump jump plough. The invention of Vegemite in 1923 showed the same quality with its skilful use of yeast left over from making beer, the national drink.

The opposing myth of the stereotypical Australian, that he's simply lazy, didn't emerge in the 1960s but has a much longer pedigree. Daniel Healey, in his book *The Cornstalk, his Habits and Habitat* of 1893, began an anecdote on his character: 'The typical Cornstalk is naturally indolent and easy going, but capable of great exertions when roused'. The story that follows describes a 'Lazy match', between an Englishman, an Irishman, a Scotsman and a Cornstalk, each trying to be the most lazy. Cornstalk's 'unfathomable laziness', of course, gives him the victory. But in the anecdote, this significantly takes the form of refusing even to enter the contest. This is called laziness by the judges, but could equally well be seen as superior common sense. Norm, of the 'Life Be In It' campaign, is a modern successor to the Cornstalk, sitting with his tinny in front of the TV. This campaign was based on a real problem, the sedentariness of the urban Australian male, and its aim was benign, to get such people to do more exercise. Yet it also confirms a stereotype of Australians (especially Australian workers—Norm doesn't look at all like a top executive) that sees them as lazy, self-indulgent and undisciplined, and in need therefore of a tough management, which will try to extract an honest day's work out of them while resisting wage claims that could hardly be justified coming from such a feckless workforce.

The Australian accent, in the broad sense of the word, is saying the same kind of thing by the same means as the accent in the narrow sense. And though the means may seem trivial, what the accent says is of the greatest importance, dealing with primary social values as these are embedded in the minutiae of everyday life. There is no need to romanticise these values in order to see them as a major cultural achievement. They are not vanishing or obsolete, dangerous or ridiculous, as middle-class parodists and moralists have been proclaiming for a century. It isn't the case that these values have been given free rein in the past, to the nation's cost. On the contrary, they were opposed then as they are now, at the same time as the energies they represented were made over and exploited. But cultural surgery exercised on the Australian accent and the Australian national character has never really been an option. The only way ahead for Australia and for Australians is to understand these values and try to work with them.

Works Referred to in the Text

Althusser, L. (1971) *Lenin & Philosophy*, London: New Left Books
Altman, D. (1980) *Rehearsals for Change*, Sydney: Fontana/Collins
Barthes, R. (1973) *Mythologies*, London: Paladin
Barthes, R. (1975) *The Pleasure of The Text*, (trans. R. Miller) New York: Hill and Wang
Barthes, R. (1982) *Empire of Signs* (trans. R. Howard), New York: Hill and Wang
Bennett, T. *et al* (1984) *Formations of Nation and People*, London: RKP
Berger, J. (1972) *Ways of Seeing*, London: BBC
Bolton, G. (1981) *Spoils and Spoilers*, Sydney: Allen and Unwin
Bourdieu, P. (1980) 'The Aristocracy of Culture' (trans. R. Nice) *Media, Culture and Society*, No. 2
Boyd, R. (1963) *The Australian Ugliness*, Melbourne: Penguin
Connell, R.W. (1977) *Ruling Class, Ruling Culture*, Melbourne: Cambridge Univ. Press
Conway, R. (1971) *The Great Australian Stupor*, Melbourne
Copping, B. and Turner, G. (1983) 'The Australian View of Art' *Australian Journal of Cultural Studies*, Vol. 1, No. 2, pp. 150–63
Coward, R. (1984) *Female Desire: Women's Sexuality Today*, London: Paladin
Fiske, J. (1983) 'The Discourses of TV Quiz Shows, or School + Luck = Success + Sex' *Central States Speech Journal*, Vol. 34, No. 3, pp. 139–50
Fiske, J. and Watts, J. (1985) 'Video Games: Inverted Pleasures' *Australian Journal of Cultural Studies*, Vol. 3, No. 1, pp. 89–103
Greenfield, P. (1984) *Mind and Media*, London: Fontana
Hancock, W.K. (1961) *Australia*, Brisbane: Jacaranda
Hodge, R. and Tripp, D. (1986) *Children and Television*, Cambridge: Polity Press
Horne, D. (1964) *The Lucky Country*, Melbourne: Penguin
Hughes, R. (1970) *The Art of Australia*, Melbourne: Penguin
Levi-Strauss, C. (1966) *The Savage Mind*, London: Wiedenfeld and Nicholson
Levi-Strauss, C. (1969) *The Raw and The Cooked*, London: Cape
McGregor, C. (1967) *Profile of Australia*, Melbourne: Penguin
McKernan, M. (1980) *The Australian People and The Great War*, Melbourne: Nelson

McQueen, H. (1975) *A New Britannia*, Melbourne: Penguin

McQueen, H. (1978) *Social Sketches of Australia 1888–1975*, Melbourne: Penguin

McRobbie, A. (1984) 'Dance as Social Fantasy' in McRobbie, A. and Nava, M. (eds) *Gender and Generation*, London: MacMillan

Mills, A. and Rice, P. (1982) 'Quizzing the Popular' *Screen Education*, No. 41, pp. 15–25

Pascoe, R. (1979) *The Manufacture of Australian History*, Melbourne: Oxford

Rowse, T. (1978) *Australian Liberalism and National Character*, Malmsbury: Kibble

Stephenson, P. (1969) 'The Foundations of Culture in Australia: An Essay towards National Self-Respect', in Barnes, J. (ed.) *The Writer in Australia 1856–1964*), Melbourne: Oxford Univ. Press

St. John, E. (ed.) (1985) *The Big Australian Rock Book*, Sydney: Megabooks

Stretton, H. (1970) *Ideas for Australian Cities*, Melbourne: Georgian House

Summers, A. (1975) *Damned Whores and God's Police*, Melbourne: Allen Lane

Ward, R. (1958) *The Australian Legend*, Melbourne: Oxford Univ. Press

White, R. (1981) *Inventing Australia*, Sydney: Allen & Unwin

Index